ARE YOU DROWNING?

OVERCOMING IN THE MIDST OF TRAUMA AND LOSS

JENNA SHOTMEYER

*This book is dedicated to the girl sitting
in her dorm room crying on the floor.*

Some names have been changed
for the privacy of those involved.

CONTENTS

Chapter 1

WAVES

ossing and turning, I gasped for air only to get the wind knocked out of me yet again. My ten-year-old body was caught in the riptide as I was trying to learn to face the waves. The large wave rolled my entire body in seemingly endless summersaults until it finally spat me back out on the shore. Sand, seaweed, and who knows what else stuck to my hair as it covered my face in clumps. I sat up and parted my hair so I could see where I was. I sighed. I was far from where I started. I squinted farther out and saw my dad and brother waving back at me.

"Come on back out!" they called in the distance.

It might seem strange that my father called for his child to come back out into the relentless waves of the sea, but there was a good reason. He was trying to teach my brother, Jacob, and me to never fight the waves.

In my father's words, "The ocean will always win. You will never be stronger than it, no matter how hard you try. People drown because they fight it. Learning to move with the ocean will keep you safe, even if it means going the opposite direction of where you want to go."

It was an essential lesson for us as we became old enough to swim in deeper parts of the ocean. If my brother or I got caught in a riptide, fighting against it would be ineffective; we'd lose energy quickly and risk the chance of drowning. The riptides on the New Jersey shoreline are notably strong, and moving *with* the ocean seems counterintuitive, which is why it seems each year someone passes away in the surf. Allowing the sea to move us in a different direction can be the right thing to do. This lets us rest and recover for when the riptide eventually lets us go, and we can move where we need to.

It would be nearly a whole decade before that ten-year-old girl would learn that this lesson was not just about swimming. Years after that moment on the beach, something happened that changed my life forever: I found myself caught in a riptide that nearly pulled me under.

I always believed I would be a stronger person if I didn't give up on exactly where I wanted to go in life. I always thought strength and dedication meant chasing my dreams and achieving my goals, regardless of the obstacles life throws at me. But the ocean taught me how different strength and commitment could look in the face of life's challenges. I was taught to have peace when the waves move me, instead of dying in a struggle against the roaring sea.

I listened and respected the words of my earthly father and even more so the words of my heavenly father—I've always ached and longed to please them both. I knew they wanted the best for me, and out of love and respect, I was determined to give my all to everything I did. At the beginning of my freshman year of college, I remember frequently singing the words of *Oceans* by Hillsong United with my hands raised high in the air: "When oceans rise, my soul will rest in your embrace." As I sang, I embraced all things new, continually committing my life to God on my brand-new college campus and this exciting phase of my life.

Chapter 2

WHO WAS I?

September was warmer than usual in 2013. Showing no intention of slipping away from summer's grasp, the sun continued to shine just like in August. I loved every moment of it, thriving in both the sunrays and in my new stage in life. I recently moved into my freshman dorm room with one of my best friends from high school. It was a dream come true.

I was on an academic scholarship and could not wait to get into my accounting and finance classes. Although most people seem to hate math, I was always the exact opposite. I loved math because it made sense to me. Unlike most everything else in the world, math was something that tended to stay the same. It was steady, a matter of fact, and exact, which made working through equations feel almost peaceful in my mind. So while my friends bemoaned their math homework, I devoured it. In fact, it was my dream since the fourth grade to be an accountant. From a young age, I had my life logically planned out, and just like the straight lines on the Excel sheet, there was a clear, straight path toward my future.

Within the first few days of my freshman year, I joined the accounting club, the physics club, and many social clubs. Joining every club that piqued my interest might have seemed overambitious, but I thrived on a busy schedule filled with hard work. Since I needed to choose a minor in order to meet the 150 credits that my CPA degree required, I considered studying physics as well. My goal was to finish 150 credits by the time I was a first-semester senior so that I would have the second semester of my senior year to study for the CPA exam. My school had a program for second-semester, CPA-bound seniors, and despite being on campus for only a week, I had already discussed this plan at length with faculty.

My work ethic was ingrained in me from a young age. Everyone I knew in my hometown in Bergen County, New Jersey, worked and played hard. I grew up in a place where there wasn't a lot of room for a bad grade or a failed test. If you slipped in your performance just a bit, there was always someone just behind you, ready to swoop in and take your spot. It was important to get good grades in middle school, to get into a good high school, to get into a good college. Everything counted, and nothing was small enough to just shrug off.

Of course, my parents tried to raise me to believe my worth wasn't based on what I accomplished, but the realities of the world were always there. If I wanted to achieve my goals, I had to work hard and push myself. I looked forward to college and the years of being a young professional the same way some of my friends would look forward to finding the perfect spouse or starting their family. I was certain these years would be the best and most rewarding of my life.

I happily took the plunge into college, which was naturally the first step in achieving my dreams. I dove into my professional development as soon as I unpacked my suitcase.

Each fall, the business school hosted Accounting Night. Firms from across the country would come to network with the students.

For freshmen, it was an opportunity to get our names out there, while students further along in their college careers used the events to score jobs and internships.

I put on my best black pencil skirt, blazer, heels, and red lipstick. I looked in the mirror and stopped myself before harsh criticisms started forming in my mind; I reminded myself I was on my way to becoming the best version of me. Nothing was going to stand in my way—I was going to rock Accounting Night! I knew my personality was made for events like this. I was very outgoing in social situations, and I was a people pleaser to the core. I was confident in my tried and true work ethic but always willing to yield to leadership. I was ready to step up when needed without having to be in charge of everything.

I took a deep breath and made my way to the auditorium. I had a stack of resumes detailing my high school accomplishments in the National Honors Society, the math club, varsity tennis, and volunteering, as well as a list of internships in politics and finance longer than some graduating college seniors. My dreams were right there within reach, and I had everything I needed to make them a reality.

Each student was told to meet in the auditorium before the night would start. I scanned the room to see if I saw anyone from my Financial Accounting class, and without seeing any of my new friends, I took a seat by myself. In the adjacent room, all of the accounting professionals were set up with large poster boards, business cards, and trinkets with the name of their firm.

I did my homework on which firms would be there and put on my best smile. I walked up to each of the men in charge of hiring for the firms and shook their hands with my firmest grip. "Hi, I'm Jenna Shotmeyer, and I am passionate about accounting. I am a freshman this year. I am a very hard worker as you can see from my resume." I felt a combination of both brave and assured as I smiled and handed each person at the table a resume. "I would love the opportunity to work my hardest for your firm."

"Wow," many replied with a chuckle and a similar answer after that: "I've never heard someone say they are passionate about accounting. We don't hire freshmen, but here's my card; let's stay in touch."

I left the auditorium that night happier than I had ever been. I began to think I was finally turning into everything I dreamed I would be, and I was right on track to achieve this mystical "future me" who was awesome. I wasn't there yet, as my insecurities crept up my throat, but I felt like I could really start to see that awesome version of myself just off in the distance.

The night felt like a success, and afterward, I called my boyfriend of just a few months to tell him all about Accounting Night. The two of us had an air of commitment to one another but the ease of being young and free. He was easy going but confident. I often joked that if I could have downloaded computer software to create any boyfriend, I would have tried to create exactly him, from his mind and faith to even his height and build. Unsure of what our relationship would look like at schools three and a half hours apart, we continued to trust God with our future.

We had met the past March when my brother invited a few freshmen college friends to my 18th birthday party. It was the end of their college's spring break, and a few of his friends were left on campus with nothing to do. Matt from Nashville and I hit it off almost instantly. It was only a matter of weeks before our first date and a couple of months before he accompanied me to my senior prom.

We didn't text very much, but I preferred talking on the phone anyway.

"Hey, how'd it go tonight?"

"Ugh, it was AMAZING! I finally feel like I am where I am supposed to be," I exclaimed as I continued to gush about the night.

I loved how Matt and I tried to support each other, but to me, the best part of our phone calls was the mental sparring. He was an engineer and finally someone who could give me a run for my money on one-liners, puns, and jokes. I loved that I had to concentrate and really think about each sentence he said in case there was hidden humor so that I could easily flip something back to him. Our fun, competitive spirit felt like a point played in tennis, which was no doubt our favorite sport.

Both of us played for our respective colleges. Matt, a budding nationally-ranked star, and I with a clean slate trying to make my own mark.

It had been my dream to make the tennis team in college since I was a freshman in high school. At the time, it felt like a lofty goal, but I practiced almost every day and worked harder than I could've imagined. Years of heat exhaustion from summer tennis camp could tell you how hard I pushed myself to play on this team. I contacted the coach years before I applied so that I would be on his radar. This was the school I wanted to be at, and this was the team I wanted to play for.

When I finally got to campus, I was the first one to arrive at the women's practice. Hitting serves and running sprints afterward, I would often not leave until after the men's practice, which followed the women's. I wanted the coach to know how serious I was—that I was prepared to be the best, most hardworking player he ever had. Maybe I wasn't the strongest, the fastest, or the most naturally talented on the team, but I could prove I was willing to work the hardest. I was fighting for worth on the team with all that I had, and I knew I would earn it.

Our first match was an hour and a half away, and I beat my opponent 6-4, 6-4. My coach was able to see what I was capable of in a match setting. The points lasted for many shots, and my senior opponent pushed me to my limits. We showed our teams what we were capable of, while cheers and whispers from onlookers, all impressed by our game, filled the court. A few of the guys on our men's tennis team told my coach how they were on the same team as my opponent in high school. They were blown away by our match and, more specifically, my victory.

Three weeks into college seemed like a lifetime. School was no longer about what I did—it was who I was. I had new friends and a whole new life of which I loved every second. I loved my independence and freedom. I loved my newfound schedule and all I could accomplish in a day. No one did more than me, and I took pride in that fact. I loved my challenging academics and extracurriculars, and I loved how I was able to physically exert myself at the gym and at tennis practice.

I put a lot of stock in my achievements, goals, and in pushing myself to be the best, which I saw in tandem with my relationship with God. I took Colossians 3:23 to heart: "Whatever you do, work at it with all your heart, as working for the Lord, not for human masters." I did everything for Him. I knew that God would use my strengths to further His kingdom. I also knew I had a very large wet blanket of insecurity entrapping me, which was far from holy. Past hurt, pain, and fear were not only in that blanket, but I knew getting rid of them was part of my life-long sanctification process. Still, God was always the center for me, and He was the center of my small college campus. I had a desire to do well at school and in life, not just because I wanted a long list of accolades, but because I wanted to use my talents and gifts to the best of my ability for the Kingdom of God. My greatest goal was to be told, "Well done, good and faithful servant" (Matthew 25:21) at the end of my life standing before God. To me, this meant trying my hardest and doing the most I could do with everything God had given me. All of my plans were made with God in mind.

I welcomed Jesus into my heart when I was five years old, and from that point on, I have keen memories of crying out to God while I was buried in a study session for a challenging test or after I was so sore from tennis camp that I couldn't move my legs. In those moments, I would declare the words from Isaiah 40:31: "But those who hope in the Lord will renew their strength. They will soar on wings like eagles; they will run and not grow weary, they will walk and not grow faint."

At college, it was tough to understand the tension I was feeling as I relied on Christ and His love for me while using self-hatred to propel myself to work harder. The more I hated my weakness, the harder I worked and the more I was able to succeed. I knew it wasn't healthy, but living in discontentment of my weakness seemed to fuel my success. It was a reliable method that actually worked for most of my life before college. But I didn't want to do that anymore. I knew that mindset wasn't from God, so I began to work on it during those first weeks of freshman year.

I knew God was real and in control of my life, and I felt confident I understood where He was leading me. Still, every time I prayed during those first few weeks of school, I felt as though God was calling me closer to Him. Though I was confident I knew what my future was supposed to be, I felt the need to continuously pray to be in His will. I cried out to God, asking Him where I should go and what He wanted me to do. It was confusing to me because college was a huge, new change in my life and an entirely new environment. In my mind, there was no other place I could be called to right then, so I imagined that God wanted me to surrender so my heart would be ready to do something great for Him on campus. I didn't know exactly what He was trying to teach me, but I was ready to find out what He was preparing for me—or what He was preparing me *for*.

Little did I know, God was indeed preparing me for something big for His Kingdom, but it was nothing I would have ever imagined—or wished—for myself. Jesus called me to draw closer to Him so that when the waters of life began to rise and when the riptide threatened to pull me to the darkest depths forever, I could trust in Him and not sink below the waves—that even when I was being pulled far from where I thought I was supposed to be, I was still safe because God was still in control.

Chapter 3

WHAT JUST HAPPENED?

For my family and me, September 20, 2013, will go down as a date that changed our lives forever. I can't remember the start of the day, but as far as I know, it kicked off in a pretty uneventful fashion. I woke up in my dorm, went to class, ate lunch with my friends, worked out, went to tennis practice, and then headed back to my room to get ready for the Glow Light Party on campus.

The party was sure to be a fun event to help take the pressure off from the first weeks of the semester. It was hosted by the Student Advisory Group and geared toward all of the new students on campus. In the first couple of weeks, I had gone to every event I possibly could in order to meet people on campus, so there was no question whatsoever that I would be going to this one too. Everyone wore white or neon clothing to the party, and everything else in the room was pitch black, save for the soft glow of black lights which illuminated our clothing. I wore one of my best tennis skirts (it was the

only white bottom I had), a highlighter-green t-shirt from a friend
down the hall, and a pink belt from J. Crew. In the mirror, I noticed
that my lipstick matched my belt as I fixed my wavy light brown hair.

I could not have been more excited to meet as many people as I
could, but I also made pacts with my friends that we wouldn't leave
each other alone. I must've texted a half dozen or more people, who
I had met in classes and through other events, to meet me there. The
party was in the center of campus, so unless you lived off campus
(which only a few seniors did), you were most likely going to stop by.

The college had a pretty sleepy campus without a heavy party culture, so there wasn't any alcohol provided. My friends and I didn't
drink anyway, so it wasn't something we missed. It was just going
to be a fun night to dance and get to know more people on campus.

An hour and a half into the party, we were ready to go home. The
dancing was getting rougher and the crowd more excited, making
quality time with friends impossible. There is little I remember from
those final moments; I just remember that one second, my friends
and I were on the dance floor, and the next, there was one of the loud-
est crashes I had ever heard.

BOOM!

It was so loud; my first thought was that a bomb had gone off and
we were all going to die. Then, searing pain shot through my entire
body, and I immediately collapsed. With my eyes closed, my ears
dialed in on the panicked voices around me:

"Are you OK?"

"Is she OK?"

"What's going on?"

"How many fingers am I holding up? How many fingers am I
holding up? How many fingers am I holding up? How many fingers
am I holding up?"

I had no clarity of sight or mind. My mass confusion turned to
frustration. I was in pain, and some girl was asking me questions that
felt outlandishly difficult. I had no idea how I was supposed to tell

her how many fingers she was holding up. How was *I* supposed to know anything about *her* fingers?

I realized whatever was happening was making quite the scene, and all I could think about was getting up and getting back to my room. I tried my best to sit up and quickly realized I couldn't move. I could not pinpoint why I could not move, so I stayed where I was. The DJ approached us—with the music still blaring and the lights still off—and told us I needed to be moved outside because I was taking up too much room on the dance floor. Still unable to move by myself or even sit up on my own, a few guys picked me up off the floor and brought me outside.

Everyone kept asking me what happened and how I was doing, but I had no idea. I felt so confused and incredibly embarrassed. There is a haze to my memory of the night and to my vision at the time. I kept trying to get back to my room, but when student paramedics came to check my vitals, they suggested I head to the hospital.

I was so perplexed—I was fine! The feeling of not wanting to be the freshman who got carted off to the ER in an ambulance right off the bat in her first semester burned within me. I didn't want to rack up tons of medical bills for an injury that wasn't that bad at all. I felt like I could be stronger than whatever had happened. If only I could sleep. I was sure I would be fine after I slept.

I gathered from those around me that people had been throwing water off the balcony, and someone threw an entire cooler over the edge that landed squarely on my head. I didn't have a chance to process any more information about the event because the student paramedics kept peppering me with questions as they flashed their painfully bright flashlights in my eyes.

"What's your address?"

I quickly answered, feeling more frustrated and embarrassed by the second. I could tell they were questioning my intelligence.

"That's not her address," one of my best friends from high school stated with deep concern in her voice.

Shaking my head, I replied, "Yes, it is. Stop it. I'm fine, really." Out of anyone, I would know my *own* address, right?

"What's your student ID number?"

Without skipping a beat, I rattled off my long student ID number. The group was shocked.

"Isn't she a freshman? She's got to be fine if she can remember that. It's only been a couple of weeks," one of the paramedics said.

"Seriously, I'm fine. Can I go back to my room now, please? I just want to sleep," I replied, absolutely frustrated with the entire conversation.

The paramedics conceded. One of the campus police officers made me sign a form that said I wouldn't be taking an ambulance to the hospital. I signed it quickly and headed back to my dorm.

My memories from the night are like loose shapes, drawn together into sketchy scenes, as others have tried to help me put things together. What I wouldn't find out until later is that after the cooler hit me, I actually laid unconscious on the dance floor for a while before I woke up. Despite feeling like I was speaking clearly and being very articulate, I was mumbling the entire night and being unusually difficult to deal with toward everyone around me, including my roommate and RA. I also didn't realize that I threw up in the bushes on the way back to my dorm, and, most chillingly, the officers told my RA to wake me a few times in the night because it was possible I wouldn't wake up ever again in the morning if she didn't.

Those around me saw a cause for concern, but as I finally got into bed that night, I was just happy for the events of the evening to be over. I rarely ever get angry, but that night was different. My RA did wake me up a few times, as did my roommate. But each time, I desperately wanted to be left alone.

I really had no idea that my life was forever changed.

Chapter 4

WHAT IS WRONG WITH ME?

The next morning, I gathered myself in my twin XL Vera Bradley bedding. A thought bounced around in my head, which was still swimming from the night before. *I have to text Matt.* I did not have the ability to call my boyfriend the night of the party, and he might wonder why. I also had this underlying feeling of guilt that I needed to tell my family what had happened to me. I always told my mom *everything*. My brother also had some friends who went to my school, and my roommate knew my family well. I didn't want them to hear what happened from someone else on the off chance someone from school communicated with my family. I wanted them to know I was OK.

Sitting up was unreasonably hard, but I didn't let myself think about that. I was focused on my goal. I grabbed my phone from the end of my bed and saw only squiggly lines on the screen. Unable to read them, I unlocked my phone and began to text my family. I relied on muscle memory to text them, so reading the squiggly lines wasn't necessary. I just needed to let everyone know what was going on. The text I sent was something like, "Hey, I got hit on the head last night, but I think I'm OK."

I began to contemplate what to text Matt next. I sighed, wishing I could read texts I thought might be from him, but they were all still squiggly lines. For whatever reason, I was not alarmed that I couldn't really read even though I had never in my life experienced such a thing. My mind convinced me this was just a challenge to overcome, and I accepted it. I was too confused and in too much pain to put together that this was an enormous issue. Ultimately, I decided to wait and call my mom to talk about Matt, but after reading my text, she was already calling me.

"Hey Mom."

"Jenna, are you OK?" Her voice faded into a blur. She started asking me insurmountably difficult questions about my text. The questions felt impossible to answer, and she was getting me off-topic. I had to concentrate on why I called, but trying to recall my reason for calling her felt nearly impossible. *Wait, was I the one to call her, or did she call me?* My memory felt incoherent, and thinking about more than one thing at a time made my mind go into overload.

Suddenly, I remembered. Matt! I had to text Matt. I did not want to talk about what seemed to be an invasively in-depth conversation covering every minute and crazy detail of my life.

"What happened to you? Are you hurt? Is everything OK? You were hit? What hit you?"

My mom sounded worried, but I couldn't wrap my mind around the depth of what she was saying. Instead, I tried to answer her questions quickly so I could get back to the topic.

"I told you, I got hit on the head. I think…I…I…I…wait, what did you ask me?" I bit my lip and frowned as I tried to articulate my thoughts, but I couldn't. "That's not why I called." I shut my eyes and shook my head slightly, trying to figure out the magnitude of how hard it was to talk. I rattled out the best I could, "Matt is in a tennis tournament, and I wanted to call him but don't want to alarm him because I'm OK. Should I just text him that I got hit on the head? I don't want him to worry before he goes on court. I just don't know what to do…" I tried not to slur and mess up my words, but the harder I tried, the more it kept happening. What was *wrong* with me? Maybe I just needed more sleep. I was exhausted and didn't feel right, but I was sure I would be fine after I slept.

Instead of answering *my* questions, she kept questioning *me*, "Why couldn't you call him back last night? What do you mean you can't read his text? Why not? Is something wrong with your phone, or is it you? What hit you on the head? Who saw it happen?"

I attempted to answer, but my mind was paralyzed by the complexity of the conversation. I slurred some pleasantries together and told her I had to go.

I have relentless determination ingrained in me, so even in my dazed state I forced myself to admit I was fine.

My head was in a fog thicker than pea soup, but my body seemed to know I needed help. I left the dorm and tried to find someone who could help me. The health center at the school was closed on weekends which left me unsure of what to do next. Talking or walking made me so tired I could barely move, but I kept going toward the athletic training facility where I imagined there would be a trainer on duty.

When I got close to the athletic buildings, I realized that no one seemed to be around. I was desperately looking for someone to help as I wandered the halls.

"Jenna! Hey!" A wrestler from my freshman seminar course yelled from across a long hallway. "Are you OK? I heard what happened to you last night! Such a crazy story! Everyone's talking about it."

"I'm trying to find the trainer," I replied.

"Yeah, of course you are. Let me take you to him; he is at the wrestling match."

He walked me to the match to talk to the trainer on duty. Everyone who had a concussion as an athlete had to go through him to get cleared. I finally felt like I was in the right place.

"Hey, this is my friend Jenna." His words mushed together in my mind amidst all of the hype and excitement around me from the match. I was thankful I had this friend as an advocate of sorts.

The trainer was either too busy to talk to me or didn't understand my problem, and I really wanted to get out of the huge room full of people. The movements, noises, colors, and words blurred around me, making me weak to the point of almost collapsing. I didn't recognize this as related to the accident the night before, and it felt so foreign to me. I left to get back in bed as soon as possible, deciding that sleep could fix this problem.

I have small snippets of memories and stories from that time. My friend brought a few meals to my bedside. I was confused and wasn't quite sure what was going on, but those deliveries at least helped me understand it was time for food. I tried to articulate how I was feeling, but the only word I could come up with was "confused." Looking back, it was so much more than that. I was baffled and bewildered by everything that happened around me. I felt disconnected from the world, and I was flustered and muddled in the midst of social interactions I normally wouldn't have to think twice about. The easiest questions sent me into a mental tailspin, and my ability to follow a simple train of thought or back-and-forth conversation was almost completely gone. I had tunnel vision that allowed my mind to focus on only one thing at a time, causing sounds, lights, and movements to leave me feeling unsteady and overwhelmed.

The strangest part was not being able to comprehend that I was experiencing those things. All I knew was that something was different; something felt wrong. I desperately wanted to be OK, so I told myself I was.

Sometime later, I went to the cafeteria for some food with my friends. I was doing my best to function despite a cyclone of dizziness so intense I was at constant risk of falling down. My thoughts were muddled, too, and I couldn't process them well enough to speak. Everything around me needed to be perfectly still in order for me to function at any level. The unexpectedness of even the smallest of movements, like a friend reaching for their jacket, made me uneasy.

As I stepped farther and farther into the cafeteria, I suddenly became even more uneasy. It seemed like a lot of people were looking at me. The attention felt frustrating, uncomfortable, and a little scary. Still, I kept walking and told myself it was all in my head. My mind was buzzing in disarray, trying to balance the growing anxiety in the pit of my stomach and the terrifying feeling that I could topple over at any moment. With my heart racing, I tried my best to focus on heading to our table.

However, my plan was interrupted when a guy I didn't know and had never seen before called out my name from behind me.

"Uh, hi! Jenna!" he said.

I knew I had to turn to face him, but turning my head meant moving out of my balanced "sweet spot" that kept me upright. Slowly and carefully, I turned toward his voice. The wind rushed in my ears as I felt my grip on my balance slip more and more precariously from me. I needed to sit down, and I wasn't about to collapse in front of some stranger (if I could help it).

"Hi," I said quickly as I tried to rush off. The way he spoke to me made me feel like I should know him, but I hadn't seen him before in my life. More concerned about not toppling over before I made it to my seat, I decided he must be talking to a different Jenna from my class and turned back around.

I felt like I was in one of those video games where you have to jump from small platform to small platform to be safe. Moving was a dangerous and delicate operation, and I wasn't safe as long as I stood. I needed to find something to lean on or somewhere to sit right away. But despite desperately needing to find my seat, wishing I could just switch into hyper-speed, I felt like I was moving in slow motion like a sprinting snail. Everyone was rushing around me, and there was nothing I could do about it.

While I attempted to make a beeline for our table, not even fully processing that I was so dizzy, I realized the guy was following me. He even started running for a few steps to get in front of me so I couldn't run off. What could be so important that it would stop me from saving myself from a humiliating tumble?

"Wait!" he yelled to me as he tried to block my escape. "Will you go to the Homecoming dance with me?"

That was what was so important? My mind was swimming. I felt sick but did not know why. And now, I was a little freaked out because this guy I had never met just asked me to a dance.

Overwhelmed by it all, I exclaimed, "What?! No! I've never seen you before in my life!" I started crying in exasperation, something very atypical of my personality.

I couldn't even process his question fully nor feel any form of flattery. All I could think about was sitting down so I could get the world around me to become as still as possible. Why was my confusion over this guy's invitation so strong that I cried? I hated that he had asked me that when I was just trying to get to my seat. I couldn't figure out why I was having such an intense reaction. I wasn't sad. Why was I so upset? Why was I so incredibly confused? Why was everything making me feel like I was on the deck of a ship in a storm? There was SO MUCH NOISE. People talking, chairs scratching against the floor, utensils clanging on plates—it was all too much. I could not even process my own questions. I wanted the attention off of me and off of me NOW. Maybe if something could divert everyone's focus, there would be less movement, fewer people trying to talk to me, and I could get back to my bed sooner.

My friends were looking at me with concern in their eyes, a bit shocked by my uncharacteristically harsh reaction.

"Jenna, isn't he the same major as you?" A girl at my table asked as I lowered my head just enough to see only my food and nothing else moving around me. I could feel a slight visual reprieve from all the commotion. "Yeah Jenna, he lives in our building! You have to know him! Our building is so small."

I didn't know him. Maybe he did live in my building, but I couldn't recall ever seeing him before. I just wanted people to leave me alone. My friends kept insisting that I knew him, which made me more and more agitated. Wouldn't I know best who I knew and who I didn't know? Why couldn't they leave me alone about this? Their questions made me feel crazy, but apart from just needing to sit down in a quiet, dark room, I felt fine, and my mind was working like normal. Couldn't they just believe me when I told them who I did and didn't know?

My friends' questions felt like relentless bugs gnawing at my face. I did not want that kind of attention; I was not asking for it. I misread their concern for me as incessant agitation. They all seemed to know things I didn't, and I wasn't used to that. It bothered me and made me want to work and push my body harder to catch up, but each word came to me in a chaotic mess. I couldn't even process the individual letters, let alone the sentences themselves. It was like forming phrases from alphabet soup in the middle of a real-time conversation.

I was no longer able to prioritize the voices of my friends over the ambient noises in the room. Every single sound felt like it was blaring at full volume in my ears. It was all too much, and I finally made it back to the almost-quiet dorm as I watched the sun set on a foggy, fragmented day.

I went in and out of murky sleep cycles where time seemed to stand still and somehow also flash by. I am not sure how long I slept, but a woman who worked for the school eventually showed up at my door. My parents had called her. They had met her at an event and wanted her to take me to a doctor. They had no idea if I was OK or seriously injured, so they decided to intervene. I didn't want to go, but I knew I owed it to my parents, who kept calling me. It was too tough to talk and answer their questions, so I had been dodging their calls, which I had never done before in my life. I wanted to talk to them and explain everything, but I wasn't sure what to explain.

I did not like the idea of a random woman bringing me to get the help I wasn't sure I wanted, but a doctor could potentially tell me what I was doing wrong so I could get stronger and get back to feeling like I was in control. I could be stubborn and make my parents even more worried, or I could put a smile on my face and please those around me. Even in that state, it was my goal to please people, so I willingly went with a smile, thanking the woman for doing me this favor. She brought my roommate and me to an urgent care center about a half-hour away.

I waited on the cold table, and Dr. Frank walked in.

At first glance, I thought he was so great. He was an older man with white hair and a loving personality, like a nice grandpa. I felt safe. I felt like I was going to get help. I wanted to be OK but couldn't figure out how to be, and I was sure Dr. Frank would be able to suggest something. I started to relax as I told myself he would tell me everything was going to be OK.

"Wow," he muttered as he kept doing strange tests on my eyes which made them hurt worse than ever.

He looked at me with a disheartened gaze, but I was comforted by his concern for me.

"Well, Jenna…This is quite unsettling," he said as he shook his head.

"What? Why? What do you mean?" I blurted out. I was very taken aback.

I wasn't sure what I did wrong to perform so poorly. I figured he could just do the tests again, and things would look better, like studying to retake a failed test in school. But trying again didn't seem to be an option. Dr. Frank didn't like something my eyes were doing, and I apparently said "yes" to the wrong ailments and "no" to things that would've eased his mind.

I knew the doctor was trying to help me, but I just wished I could say the right things that would make him and everyone else stop worrying. Ultimately, if everyone else stopped worrying about me, I wouldn't have to worry either.

"Jenna, you've had a very severe concussion, and I'm going to have to send you to the hospital immediately." I thought that was bad, but then he told me I would need to take at least two weeks off from tennis. He started writing down notes, occasionally looking up at me with great concern. He continued to emphasize my time off from tennis. No practice, no matches, nothing. A complete and total break. It was a punch in the gut. His words trailed off in my mind.

I wanted him to shut up. My mind was in chaos like a nest of spiders just being born, going in so many directions faster than I could comprehend. Every word made my body shake and anxiety scream within me. I no longer felt safe. I was almost too confused to panic… almost.

Externally, I began to shake uncontrollably as I internally shouted, "PLEASE SHUT UP. STOP TALKING. PLEASE, DR. FRANK, STOP TALKING YOU CANNOT BE RIGHT. STOP. PLEASE STOP."

I had been so certain that Dr. Frank would tell me everything was fine and that there was a quick and easy way to fix how weird I had been feeling. People would stop knowing things I didn't know, and everything would go back to normal. I never imagined that this would affect tennis. If he wanted to send me to the emergency room right then, maybe I *wasn't* OK. What would it mean if something more serious was wrong? How long would I have to stay in the hospital? I didn't need to go to the emergency room, right? If I hadn't gone to the hospital a few days ago when the injury happened, why should I go now? What could they really do for me anyway? I did not want to let that happen. I absolutely would not let those words he had just said about tennis be true. A serious head injury would, to put it lightly, place a serious damper on my second tennis match to be played the following weekend. I knew I could overcome the confusion I felt. I reasoned that I could walk, so I was *fine*. Who was he to say I was not OK? I could suppress the weakness.

My words were pasted into phrases as I had lost my ability to express myself. All I could say were things like,

"Umm…what?"

"I mean… "

"Not right."

"This…no!"

I was flooded with emotion. My eyes teared up, and he knew that I was shocked and petrified by his prognosis. I was not able to think about the possible implications of my injury; I was just zoned in on how it would affect smaller problems like tennis, which felt so huge at the moment. I felt betrayed by him. I thought he was on my team, and being on my team meant I could go back to bed soon, not go to the hospital. Being on my team meant telling me I was going to be OK and back to normal in no time.

I didn't just *think* I couldn't take two weeks off of tennis; I *knew* I couldn't.

Strong, hurtful thoughts lingered in the back of my mind about missing even one match. Anyone who knows sports knows a new freshman will be overlooked if they stop showing up. The team will not just play the match with your spot open; it *will* be filled. My mind reeled. Perhaps it would be filled by someone better than me; then, I won't be needed when I come back. If I stop working out and practicing for two weeks, I won't be at the top of my game, which I needed to be to secure my place. I was a college athlete. What would I be without that identity, even for those weeks? Of course, there is a big difference between not showing up and having a serious injury, but what doesn't change is the fact that life would still happen with or without me being there. I needed to be there to prove that I had worth to my team and prove to myself that I had worth as a person. I failed. I was failing myself, my team, and my entire support base of my friends and family by missing these two weeks. This meant I had to think enough positive thoughts to push myself to be the healthiest I could be as quickly as possible.

Tearing myself away from my thoughts, I looked back up at the doctor. Dr. Frank's eyes sparkled like the old, kind grandpa I imagined he was as my eyes continued to flood with unwanted tears. He reassured me that tennis was not what I was supposed to be upset about in this kind of situation. With one last compassionate nod, Dr. Frank left the room. I slid my shaking legs off of the still-cold table, keeping my eyes locked on the floor, in part for stability but mostly to hide the tears that had begun to fall down my cheeks.

I arrived at the hospital with my roommate. Even though I had her with me, I felt so alone. Adult-like freedom was no longer as great as it seemed, and I wished I had my mom. Not only would she help me handle the paperwork I would no doubt have to struggle through filling out, but she would help me tell myself I was OK. She would say to me that we would figure it out and that the worst would be over soon. It was just weeks ago that I barely left our house without her knowing where I was going. Now I was checking myself into an emergency room, in an unfamiliar city, without her.

I cradled my license, insurance card, and credit card in my hands as I cautiously walked up to the dull, brown counter to check myself in. I didn't feel brave; I felt numb and fragile.

"Hi, I'm Jenna Shotmeyer. Umm, I was hit on the head, and they sent me here."

I sat down on the fake leather seats in the cold and outdated waiting room. My phone buzzed in my pocket, to my dismay. I wanted this nightmare to end. I wanted it all to stop: the texts, the comments, the doctor's orders to stay away from tennis. It was all too hard to respond to and process, and I desperately wanted this narrative to be over.

I tried to process the situation the only way I knew how—making light of it all. My roommate and I took some pictures of my unamused face in the emergency room and posted them to get people to stop making a big deal of what happened. I wanted it to stop being a topic of conversation. The best way to do that was to share that I was

OK, show I could laugh it off, and move on. I was barely answering texts, and everyone was on social media: Snapchat, Instagram, Facebook. If I could post something, it would show I was healthy, and the picture itself could answer the texts I had been getting. Deep in my gut, I felt that if I kept telling myself I was OK, I *would* be OK. If I kept silent from my friends, it would prove I couldn't handle what had happened.

I was so tired, and I had to go in to see the ER doctor alone. It was oddly difficult to walk as I made my way from the emergency room to the back. Would they keep me overnight? I was shaking but did not know why. If only I could sleep. I complained of head and stomach pain to the nurses who asked so many questions. I felt so frustrated at how confused I had been. I was always mentally in control of myself, so why was this so different?

I sat there in a cold bed, in a dank emergency room, in a big city. I was constantly hit with the cold breeze of nurses running past with stretchers, but I was out of sight in my room made with walls of sheets. The whole thing sent a shiver down my spine. I felt so alone. I didn't want to go in for a scan; those things creeped me out. Perhaps Dr. Frank was right, and I would need to be here for a while. Part of me was open to being at the hospital for a while because, admittedly, something just wasn't right. However, I wasn't sure that was the right answer, and the hospital felt just a little too dramatic for me when I couldn't even pinpoint the problem. But I still held out hope that perhaps nothing was wrong, and I would get cleared by Wednesday's practice to play my Saturday tennis match. That would be the best outcome.

The doctor came in and barely looked at me. Dr. Frank at urgent care told me to get a CT scan at the hospital to check for bleeds. That seemed like a good idea, but now this new doctor said not to. He mentioned something about the radiation being very bad for me, and he didn't think I needed it. I don't think he performed any tests, and he just half-listened to my story. But I didn't care because, if he said I was OK, I could get cleared for the match.

I kept trying to retain the information he gave me. I crinkled my nose and squinted my eyes amidst the light sensitivity as if that would help me understand better what he was saying. I knew my dad would want a full report of what happened, and the idea of trying to relay this information to him overwhelmed me. Each time the doctor repeated himself, it was as if his words were sand in my open hands, quickly escaping before I could grab hold.

I looked up at the doctor in desperation, holding my cell phone in both hands. "I don't know how to tell my parents that, so can you talk to them on the phone?"

I literally did not know how to communicate his words to my parents. Not because it would upset my parents, but it was as if my muscles and mind had never tried to relay words before. It seemed like an insurmountable task. I was surprisingly calm; I just could not figure out how I was supposed to be the person who was given the job of conveying information. That skill seemed so foreign that I did not even realize that just a few days before, I had been able to do it with no problem or hesitation.

Irritated and looking at his watch, the doctor took my phone and called my dad.

"Hello? Mr. Shotmeyer? Yes, this is the ER doctor. I'm calling about your daughter…" The rest of the conversation drifted into a gentle hum as each word disappeared in my mind as soon as it left his mouth. The only thing I remembered him saying was that I was OK.

I breathed a sigh of relief. I could stop trying to retain information. I was finally able to tune out the muffled voice of the doctor. Everyone was going to know I was OK, and I could earn my spot on my team.

Sadly, it wasn't over. My parents wanted me to follow up with the health center on campus on Monday when they opened. I woke up feeling so strange yet again, staring at the ceiling in my twin XL bed. I tried to pinpoint what felt weird or off, but I couldn't. The ER doctor said I was fine, after all. He knows more than I do, so I told myself I should have confidence that I am OK. *Get over it, handle*

it, just deal with it, OK? I would say to myself. *Don't be so dramatic.
You want to be OK, don't you? Then just be fine! You can do it.* Being
injured meant I would have to compromise on my goals. I was not
a compromiser; I was a winner. I would find a way, and I would get
cleared by the athletic trainer. I was not prepared to have this blip in
my freshman fall semester story.

I went to the center and told them what happened at the Glow
Light Party and what I could articulate of how I felt afterward. I pieced
together parts of what happened like a second grader trying to paste
pieces of a magazine onto construction paper. Too much glue, no
real point in mind, and the result looking like a mess.

As I was leaving, the woman at the front desk asked me how I
would pay for the visit.

Why would I pay for the visit? They didn't do anything for me.
It was just a simple conversation with a nurse to put everyone at
ease. It didn't feel like an appointment. Plus, I wasn't there because
I wanted to be.

On top of that, I knew my dad would have a certain way he would
want me to pay for it. He is so good with financial organization, and
I wanted to do the right thing. My mind stopped working as forming a coherent thought felt like the most daunting task in the world.
I could not isolate one idea from another to find an answer for her.

"What? Umm…pay?" I studied the nurse's face, trying to find
meaning in her expression.

"Yes," she said abruptly, in a forceful tone. "I've asked you three
times. Do you want me to put the charge on your account, or will
you pay now?"

I stood in front of her in utter confusion. What was she asking? What was I supposed to do? What would my dad want me
to do? I felt like I was on a high-speed train approaching a fork in
the tracks, not knowing which way to go. The noise of the confusion kept getting louder. What was the right thing to do? The last
thing I wanted was to have to come back and change the payment

method. I needed to get back to bed, *NOW.* I tried to speak but could not. I tried to make a decision but could not. Why couldn't I speak? I knew I had the ability. I had spoken earlier that day, right? Why could I not make a decision? The rushing kept getting louder and faster. My mind was blank. The room began to spin. Fast at first, then faster, *faster* as the confusion noise kept getting louder and louder. *Get your act together!! What is wrong with you?? Answer her!* Oh, I was so nauseous…

I must have blacked out because I found myself hysterically sobbing on the floor some time later. Heaving and shaking uncontrollably, I felt my body being picked up by someone who brought me back to the room with the nurse.

"I guess you're not OK then, huh?" The nurse said to me as I continued to heave and tried to calm myself down.

I gave my phone to the nurse to call my parents. This was the last straw for them. They dropped everything at once, packed up their car, and came to get me.

I was haunted by the feeling of not knowing what was going on. *What's wrong with you?* I kept asking myself. I was too confused and tired to be as embarrassed as I knew I should be by the scene I just made. However, I knew I could not have handled it any differently. Why was the woman at the desk so rude? Why was everyone asking me questions that were so hard?

When my parents arrived at my school, my mom gave me a big hug, and so did my dad. The ride back home was long, as even looking out the window felt utterly tiresome and draining. The usual excited chatter that filled our car turned to somber silence as talking felt like a mental calisthenic.

It was quiet at home, unlike the dorm. I hated that I was home because it felt like admitting defeat. Somehow, though, I knew I was defenseless and accepted it. My thoughts were short and fragmented, like that of poetry.

I was in and out of sleep,
For days or weeks,
I couldn't recall, for the walls
All around me had developed leaks.

The sun was clouded
By fog in my brain,
Not knowing where I was,
In sun or in rain.

In those days, I slept about sixteen to twenty hours a day. I was so tired and confused. I would wake up, try to complete a task, and then after being utterly unsuccessful, go back to sleep. I was unsuccessful at everything I tried to do. I hated how weak everything made me feel. I couldn't pinpoint what was wrong, but I also could not do anything right. I told myself that if I rested, I could go back to school.

Some people told me they would "love to be able to sleep in" when I told them how much I was sleeping. But I hated sleeping in. I hated *sleeping*, actually. "I'll sleep when I die" was my motto all throughout high school. My whole life, I had equated sleep with laziness. Sleeping twenty hours a day was then total defeat, but I couldn't do anything about it. I wasn't leisurely practicing self-care; this felt like the flu. My body needed sleep, but I was bound to my bed and hated it. This bondage was one of the most humiliating chains in my prison cell of symptoms.

Right away, we went to the highest-rated neurologist in the NYC area, and he suggested I sleep and rest, as if I needed to be told. The doctor said I would eventually wake up one day and be fine. That didn't make any sense, but there was so much that did not make sense, and I just assumed that was how concussions worked. One day you get terribly hurt, and one day you are better. I had known only one person who was not better after a few weeks from a concussion, so what would make me an exception? The doctor told me to monitor myself and that I could rest assured I would get better.

We wanted to believe him. He said most concussions cleared up before the three-month mark. Three months at first sounded like the saddest thing in the world, but we told ourselves it would not take that long. My situation was so daunting for my parents that they were quick to lean on the hope that I would resume regular life in less than three months. Of course we would believe that! We had no reason not to. It was so awful, but we could persevere. We continued to think positively and together hung on to the hope that I would wake up and be back to normal one day very soon.

Of course, we wanted to make sure we were doing everything we could to manage my symptoms and help speed the healing process. We followed up, did our homework, and saw as many doctors as we could—neurologists, primary care physicians, orthopedics doctors, chiropractors, you name it.

My mom would try to get me out of the house, deeply disturbed by my total lack of normal activities. It was a weekday morning in a quiet town—of course I could handle *that,* right? A leisurely, mother-daughter shopping trip would certainly be good for both of us.

The twenty-minute car ride to the store already made me more nauseous and disoriented than I was before. We pulled into the open-air shopping center and walked into the huge Anthropologie store encased by high ceilings and glass walls that let in a flood of natural light.

I winced amidst the assault of the sun beaming through the windows. Although beautiful, it brought on a deep ache behind my eyes. Each one of my senses was bombarded like an unexpected wave crashing into my face. Every detail of every pattern on every type of product seemed to loudly call my attention at once. I was unstable and began to realize I may fall down or throw up any second.

"Hi! Welcome to Anthropologie! Are you home from school? Where do you go?" The voice of the sales associate seemed to attack me, just like the sun's bright light.

It felt like she had just slapped me in the face with her question. Forgetting that I "should" be in school, the sales associate's innocent curiosity sent me hurling back into reality. I stared at her, took a couple of quick breaths, tried to put thoughts on an empty sheet of paper in my mind, and then lost it...

I answered her question by hysterically sobbing in the middle of the store.

I was heaving and losing all control.

"OK, OK you're OK..." My mom swiftly cradled my shaking body and confidently reassured me. "She's fine. We're good." She reassured the sales associate while whisking me out of the store to sit down on a bench outside.

I eventually gathered myself but had no answer as to what had just happened. I was sad I wasn't at school, but why was I so emotional? Why didn't I just say the name of my school?

Jenna, what is WRONG with you?? I kept asking myself. *You made a FOOL of yourself. You are so STUPID!!!*

The Anthropologie sales associate had just meant to make polite conversation, but she had uncovered a huge insecurity. Even though I was just home trying to heal, I felt like I had failed. I didn't go to school anywhere, and even when I was at home, I couldn't do anything.

We didn't go into any of the other stores that day. We just went home. The car ride was mostly silent because neither of us knew what to say. We always chatted a mile a minute, but I had no words left, and my mother was processing her own version of the confusing mess we were in.

"Today was a difficult day..." she said when she came up to my room to say goodnight as the color of the sunset had slipped back behind the trees. I took a deep breath and exhaled loudly. We both went to sleep that night with the hope that tomorrow would be better.

A few days later, I tried to bake our family's famous pumpkin-cranberry bread. I had always loved baking, and this particular recipe was a specialty of ours. I took some of the supplies out and put them on the counter, but that small task made me incredibly tired. Confused as to why that would make me tired, I pushed forward. I began the recipe and suddenly found myself, who knows how much later, holding up ingredients and wondering if they had made it into the mix. *Did I just put baking soda into the mixture?* I asked myself as I stood holding up the baking soda, utterly clueless as to whether I had put it in moments before or not. What step was I on? Why was I so tired? My eyes began to shut forcefully. Why had I forgotten? When did I start this process? I had no way of knowing if I had been standing there for ten minutes or two hours.

"I think I'm going to throw up," I muttered. I ran as fast as I could without falling until I reached the bathroom and then collapsed beside the toilet. I practically crawled back to bed, desperately not wanting to puke again from being so dizzy.

My parents promised me they would take me back to school when I was well enough to return. But that date felt further and further with every passing day. A few days at home turned into weeks, and weeks drudged into months. I was terrified of being home too long to go back to finish the semester. Initially, my mother had convinced me to come home by promising me that I could train with my old tennis coach to prepare for the upcoming spring season. Then, I wouldn't lose as much ground on my plans, as the idea of a wasted semester lingered in my mind. But since I couldn't even manage to make pumpkin-cranberry bread without feeling confused and nauseated, I thought for sure I was wasting time.

Week after week went by, and my heart sank. I was missing out on all I had planned, dreamed, and focused on for years. I felt like I was a failure to myself, my parents, siblings, Matt, friends at school, and everyone I could think of because I was too laid up to be there for them. I was a mere shadow of who I had been, and I had to get better for them as soon as humanly possible. I was missing out, and there was not one thing I could do about it.

I imagined that, like every other part of my life at the time, all of my relationships would fall apart, but two were holding on stronger than ever.

My little sister Cara has one of the most caring, beautiful hearts in the world. Before the accident, I never needed to be cared for. Our six-year age difference meant that I wanted to be the one to help her, not the other way around. Now, she was the one caring for me. She had sobbed while hugging me for about five full minutes when she dropped me off at college with my parents. Now I was back and actually *needed* the help of my twelve-year-old sister. She had all sorts of ways she would try and cheer me up. This usually involved Hannah Montana reruns, baking chocolate chip cookies, or bringing me water. We had a lot of fun together, and she quickly went from the role of baby sister to best friend. She loved being able to help me, and it made her sad that I was so hurt. I think her disappointment in my recovery and her heart-felt sympathy may have hit me more than anyone else's, although our relationship was thriving more than ever. It was so pure, and the last thing I wanted to do was continue to disappoint her.

At that point, I honestly wouldn't have blamed Matt for leaving me, but he kept coming back. Each weekend when he could have been out partying with his fraternity brothers in Hoboken, NJ, he would come to see me. In the three months we dated before the accident, each date was high-adventure as we would pop in and out of New York City and explore places we've never been. Now, even games like checkers proved to be too complicated of an activity, and we couldn't just go anywhere to eat. The few times we ventured out, Matt called the restaurant to make sure he didn't hear any loud noises in the background so it would be a quiet experience for me. My guilt compounded after every date. Was this *really* where he wanted to be on a Friday night? I felt safe with my sister on the weekend "watching" a movie as I sat backward, away from the TV because it hurt my eyes too much to actually watch it. Adding Matt to the mix meant there was a nineteen-year-old boy I really liked who was sitting with my family watching *Hannah Montana: The Movie* as I observed my family's reactions to keep up with what was going on in the scenes. I felt like I was failing him. But each time my eyes welled up with tears, Matt would affirm that next to me was his favorite place to be. I tried to understand that more than anything, but I could not shake the deep feeling of guilt that told me I owed it to him and my sister to get better. If I got better, this tough season we were in together would all be worth it. They were holding up their end of the bargain, and now I had to hold up mine. I felt like I would be able to "pay them back" and care for them somehow in the future, rather than accept the love they had for me as a gift.

If I couldn't be there for friends and family the way I wanted to in person, I thought that I at least could be present on social media. Sitting in bed, I would log onto Facebook, eyes squinting and fully focused on the post in front of me. Reading a status, I knew it didn't make any sense. So I would read it again, forcing my eyes to read on. I would look away, puzzled, wondering what in the world the person was trying to say. Eventually, I would just give up on the post, assuming it had terrible grammar. It was astounding how many friends of mine had a sudden onset of terrible grammar.

Scrolling through some more, I got an eerie feeling there were quite a few people I didn't know in my feed. I would click on a name and realize I had absolutely no idea who that person was. This wasn't just vaguely not knowing the person; I was totally blank on who these people could possibly be. I assumed someone had hacked my account and added all sorts of people I didn't know to my profile. My heart sank. Now more than ever, I wanted my safety and privacy. I began to unfriend everyone I didn't know, until I got a few messages from people who were angry with me. One guy even said I had ruined his night. Why would it ruin the night of a stranger when someone they didn't know unfriended them? I didn't know the answer and was thoroughly creeped out.

Of course, I hadn't been hacked, and my friends didn't suddenly forget how to write grammatically correct sentences after the accident. Tragically, the processing and memory shortcomings that caused my everyday frustrations also prevented me from being able to think rationally about what was happening. The truth was that I could barely read and had forgotten some combination of years of high school, including the people I knew during those abruptly-forgotten years.

Heightened by the fact that I still didn't know what was going on, I saw this unwanted season of my life as a time where I was nothing. I could do basically nothing, so I *was* nothing. I was not a student, an athlete, a friend, or any label I could think of. I had full hope that I would, one day, be worthy of loving myself again. I had complete faith that God would use this time of my life for Him and His glory. I clung to the ultimate hope that even though I *was* nothing, this was not *for* nothing.

I think people handle situations very differently when they see their struggle as an unwanted chapter of their life instead of something they will have to deal with for the *rest* of their life. Viewing my current state as only a temporary, forgettable setback opened the door for me to believe I was currently worthless. I told myself this was nothing more than a phase. I promised myself that I would very soon be back to normal and back to having worth.

Amidst the clouded confusion, I was heartbroken. The injury was dismantling the carefully laid plan I had crafted for my future. I kept telling myself I was going to go back to school as soon as possible. Initially, the tunnel vision of my mind was only concerned about my next tennis match, which expanded to the entire fall season. Now in November, I began to obsess over other details of my college experience, like my major. I had to get 150 credits by the time I graduated. Thankfully, I had already transferred a semester's worth of credits from high school dual enrollment, so it was still possible as long as I could put in a lot of work moving forward.

I had a great family I loved, only second to God, but I wanted my freedom back. I appreciated how my parents and sister did everything possible to care for me, but I wanted to be studying and experiencing college on my own. I hated feeling so out of control of achieving my dreams after so many years of hard work.

I would open my Bible from time to time and wonder why sometimes I could read a few sentences and sometimes I could not. What was preventing me from reading? My eyes were not working quite right, but I couldn't articulate what the problem was.

I made out the words in Psalm 13:1 (NKJV): "How long, O Lord?" I underlined them with my pen and wrote the date of November 2013 next to it, figuring I would one day look back and remember how difficult and painful this small, frustrating chapter was. I was bewildered and shocked that I was still home from school and struggled to put together the concrete reasons that explained why I was not OK.

My parents became exasperated. How and why had their intelligent, hard-working, athletic, and outgoing daughter turned into someone who spent most of her days bound to her bed? Doctors were not giving us solutions that were working. How could we accept that this could be my new normal?

My dad kept asking me if whatever was preventing me from reading had "cleared up." I didn't know, and I wasn't sure how to figure out *how* I could know. It wasn't an exact science, and my lack of ability wasn't as clear-cut to me as the difference between being able to read and not being able to read. I could not separate blurred vision from double vision, and although both an ophthalmologist and an optometrist reported that I had 20/20 vision, concentrating made things so much worse.

Because I couldn't articulate my reading difficulties, my dad kept checking in, asking if I was ready to go back to school (or when I thought I'd be ready). I would take a deep breath and contemplate it, hoping more than anything to be back at school. I could read for a few minutes sometimes. I could hear and concentrate on what my dad was saying for the time being. I could sit in the stillness and quietness of my living room without stuttering or slurring my words. *See? You're fine.* I would tell myself. *Why would you not be fine? You need to go back to school.*

I was resolute, so I responded to my dad's questions with all of the confidence I could muster, "I can go back. I have to go back."

I lived my life in a blur, but my ambition pushed me onward.

Head injuries are quite different than most other injuries. My MRI scans showed I had a bad injury but the doctors did not give us any indication of what the problems were or how I could be helped. Doctors would ask me how I felt to determine how bad I was. It seemed like it was up to me to determine the extent of my injury. I felt like I was, for all intents and purposes, in charge of deciding my prognosis. If I could not pinpoint what was wrong with me, it seemed like the right thing to just decide I was OK. Sure, I would fail a sports concussion screening test and probably fall flat on my face for even trying. But I wasn't at a place where I could even consider going back to sports. I was just trying to go back to class. My relentless determination and generally optimistic attitude made me decide that I was healthy.

My dad, being so similar to me, did the same thing. We decided it was a matter of positive thinking, and we believed I would be OK if I just was able to get out of the house more. I mean, it had been three whole months! I was not emotionally ready to choose not to return to school. Admitting that I was not well while knowing we had not found a solution or quick fix would've been too tough. Similarly, I don't think my dad was ready to face the devastating state of my health because the situation would be just too sad. We weren't facing realities yet, and we didn't even know what the facts were, even if we wanted to face them.

However, my mom and Matt saw right through my defense mechanisms. They saw all the things I did not. It was a precarious balance I held. I was not lying to them, the doctors, or anyone who asked me questions about my health. I was honest and sincere with what symptoms I had and what was going on. But I didn't think I was in denial. Instead, I kept a positive mindset and believed in full faith and hope that I was OK.

Still, I would have to get the go-ahead from my neurologist to return for the spring semester. No neurologist in their right mind would clear someone to return to independent living at college who was unable to stay awake more than six hours at a time, slurred her speech, and fell down multiple times a day…

Except I did get cleared by him.

I was as clear as I could be with my neurologist about my symptoms, and sure enough, he gave me the go-ahead to go back to school. Looking back, it is so hard to understand why he cleared me. Maybe he did because I followed every recounting of symptoms with a smile and, "But I really think I'm OK." Maybe it was because I presented myself with poise and had a somewhat normal conversation for a few minutes before I would deteriorate right in front of him. Maybe he assumed that I was lazy and enjoyed sleeping all day, or that I had a forgetful and ditsy personality. Maybe he thought I was exaggerating my symptoms for attention. Whatever it was, no one was going to stop me from going back to school after he gave me the green light to return.

The day I learned I would be going back to school was cloudy and cold. The lake by my house had frozen over, and Matt and I were out on the ice which was covered in hard-packed snow. We walked and talked.

Someone in my family took a photo of us with hockey sticks in our hands, as my sister had just been playing with some friends. The reality behind the cute photo was that I was not playing hockey—I could barely stand upright amidst the dizziness. But of course, Instagram would never know. We were lucky I had made it out of my house to even go for a short walk.

As we stood on the frozen lake, Matt looked at me with tears in his eyes. He began to plead with me in a soft, quiet voice, "Don't go back. Please…"

It would've been too easy to imagine that he didn't want me to go because he would miss me. It was so much easier to see him while living at home.

His eyes suggested that he would still care about me if I were on medical leave for another semester. I rejected the idea that I was worthy of love if I stayed unproductive. What's the point of sleeping eighteen hours if I'm still exhausted when I wake up? How much more did I need? I kept belittling myself as ammunition to get back to school. Without acknowledging the care that Matt expressed in his voice, I just shook my head.

"I have to go back," I told him with resolve.

I looked down and began to counteract his pleading and concern with harsh words for myself. *All of your friends are living on their own, and you are so weak. You're disgusting. Everyone is going to make friends and move on without you. You will be forgotten if you don't go back. No one will need you, and they'll think you're stupid for graduating late. You are stupid if you graduate late. How could you explain that to an employer? No accounting firm will want to hire you if you are weak like this. Everything you worked for will be all for nothing if you cannot go back. One semester is going to be hard enough to explain! How will you show your dream employer that you are strong enough to work under their intense demands if you graduate late? Pathetic!*

I needed to go back to school, and that's what I did. I was in the grasp of the riptide but was unwilling to let it move me. With every bit of strength I had, I would fight the waves.

Chapter 5

WHY IS THIS SO HARD?

t was a particularly cold winter that year. The color from my days was gone and replaced with blinding white, shades of gray, and the blackness of night. I was lost and felt like I was aimlessly trying to find my way through a thick blizzard back to my identity, purpose, and self-worth. There were heaps of snow on the ground to go along with the heaps of pressure I had put on myself.

I went back to school with the hope of a speedy recovery.

Up until that point, I knew little about what happened to me the night of the accident. The "investigation" by the school was being handled terribly and irresponsibly, but I personally stayed out of it. It was too hard to concentrate on figuring it out. I had heard only bits and pieces, like when my mom exclaimed to the Dean of Students over the phone, "How can you tell me you do not know what happened or who is responsible? What do you mean the security tapes were erased? How could there only be off-duty student RAs chaperoning hundreds of students at an on-campus party? How could my daughter be fine one minute and the next be home on our couch unable to get up with no explanation of what happened?"

A whole sports team had been questioned, as well as some other students. One freshman girl came forward to say she had done it, and it was pretty clear she was protecting her friends since it didn't seem possible it could be just her.

I knew her name and a bit of what she looked like. She was shorter than me with brown hair. The thoughts I had of her were vague and simple. I had never talked to her before, and I barely put any thought into forgiveness. It seemed like an easy offense for me to forgive because I assumed she was very sorry. Sure, it was reckless that she was goofing around with her friends in that way, so it's not surprising things got out of control. It was a mistake that I could not have seen myself making—throwing a cooler into the air? Obviously, it would hurt someone in a room packed with people. However, I assumed it tore her up inside that she had severely hurt someone and shattered their dreams for freshman year. My school had only about 3,000 students, so I expected to see her at some point, probably coming up to me with tears in her eyes carrying an apology she had thought out for four months. It puzzled me that she had not reached out to me through a written apology in the time I was home, but I assumed she had trouble finding my contact information or something. I imagined running into her on campus—maybe I would recognize her first, or she would recognize me first. Perhaps we would recognize each other at the same time. I pictured that it would be a moment of healing: we would both cry together, hug it out, and move on. I thought about it once, and that was enough for me.

I walked into my first class of the semester feeling physically terrible but also so incredibly thankful to be back at school. This class was required for every first-year student, so it had thirty-three different sections, three of which this particular professor was teaching. I chose this section based on what time of day would be best for my health. Too early would have meant my eyes were still in double-vision like they were every morning, and too late in the day would mean my body would crash so hard I would collapse to sleep afterward. It was that sweet spot around mid-morning that I could almost focus clearly.

I found a seat against the back wall so there would not be any movement behind me and rested my head on my water bottle to avoid the commotion in front of me. I found a way to control the visual overload, but I could not escape the resounding sounds of my classmates finding their seats.

From the corner of the room by the door, I heard a familiar voice call out to me.

"Jenna! Hey!" I peered up from my comfortable position and squinted my eyes. "Ugh, I'm so happy you're in this class too!" A girl with straight brown hair and the biggest smile sat down next to me.

"Krissy! YES!!" I immediately felt a sense of release and comfort that she was sitting next to me. "I'm so glad you're here!"

Krissy lived across the hall from me in the dorm. She had a kind and understanding spirit. She knew about the accident and that I was doing less than well. It meant so much to have a trusted friend with me as I felt unstable in my own body and entirely new external surroundings. The dorm was my home, and having her there was like bringing a piece of home with me to class.

The professor, who came highly recommended, walked into the class. He was an older man of short stature with grey hair and a beard. Some of the students who had taken him the semester before cheered as he smiled and began to make a few jokes.

"OK, let's take attendance and see who is here," he began. I put my head back down to try and ease the eye pain, knowing it would be a while until the professor reached my section of the alphabet. His voice hummed along with my classmates' indistinguishable chatter until I heard a name I knew I recognized.

"Meredith Jones."

My head immediately popped up.

"Here!" Someone said about two chairs down from me.

"Meredith! I saw your name on the sheet. I am so happy you are here." the Professor said and went on to mention how she was in one of his classes the previous semester.

I stopped breathing for a moment. I looked at her. Brown hair, shorter than me, and I was certain that was the name of the person who hit me.

Stunned, I sat frozen in my seat. The room rocked like a boat. My eyes struggled to focus as my mind attempted to think through the situation at hand. I quickly made a plan to rush out of class as soon as it ended to avoid having to speak with her and so I could get a few bites of lunch and head back to bed as soon as possible. Then, I began to reconsider. I remembered how I *thought* I would feel at this moment when we saw each other. I thought this would be a great day of reconciliation, but I became much more afraid than I expected myself to be. I was worried that I would not be able to concentrate and hear her apology, and I was afraid of throwing up in front of people. A whole host of other fears crept into my mind but I suppressed them. *OK, you need to do this for her. Not everything's about you. You'll need to let her talk to you. You know she is here, and she knows you are here.* I decided that I would not avoid her, but that I would take the time to release her from the horrible guilt she must feel.

I knew reconciliation with her was a large piece in the puzzle of my healing, as well as her own. I knew if the roles had been reversed, I would be crippled by guilt. The two of us would feel much better after we talked. Plus, I wanted to know once and for all what happened to me because I still didn't know for sure, and I knew it would be helpful to find out exactly how I was hit with the cooler. I half expected her to stand up right after class and come to me right away. Would we even make it out of the classroom before she apologized?

Class ended, and to my surprise, Meredith left without even so much as looking at me. My thoughts spiraled and whirled around the room, just like the room itself. I was shocked. I was actually paralyzed by how insensitive I found her choice to leave without a single glance in my direction. Looking around the room a couple of times to make sure she really, truly left, I stood there with my mouth open. I hadn't seen her walk away. She must've bolted in the opposite direction for her to be gone so fast. I knew it had to have been her; there wouldn't be someone else on campus with the same name, right? I figured she must have felt the same way about me. Even if she didn't know what I looked like, she at least knew my name.

I pushed my thoughts aside, took a deep breath, and went up to my professor's desk with a note from special services explaining my accommodations for his class. In my mind, registering with the department represented my weakness, and I hated that. However, I knew I would absolutely need to be allowed to take breaks from class, in addition to having modifications, like altered assignments. I told myself it was for just a short amount of time, and soon enough, I would be back to my old self again.

Painfully embarrassed about having to admit to yet another person that I was weak and needed help, I waited for my professor's attention.

"Um, excuse me? Professor?" I asked, feeling like a dog with its tail between its legs. During class, he seemed like such a caring person, so I expected to receive some grace and understanding. A few moments passed by, and he still hadn't looked up from his desk. I spoke again.

"Professor? Um, hi, excuse me…"

"Yes, what?" He said bluntly. His eyes darted up to meet my own, beckoning me to speak as quickly and efficiently as possible.

I continued, taken aback by his response. "Um, well, last semester, I got hit on the head with a water cooler. I had to take last semester on medical leave from school. I'm OK now, though! Well, I'm not exactly OK now. I am working with the Office of Special Services; do you know them? They said they could help because I can't really read. Well, sometimes I can read a few sentences, but then I get double vision…"

"You have a sheet to give me?" My professor set down his pen hastily and sat back in his chair, arms crossed. "You can only work with them if they give you a sheet. Only if you have a documented issue."

The phrase "documented issue" made my face turn pink from embarrassment. It seemed to imply that I had done something wrong or lost my intelligence.

"Um, yes. Here it is." Handing him the piece of paper felt like I was handing over my privacy. I was exposed and feared that he would exploit my deepest insecurities. Even though he had such a friendly demeanor during class, it seemed that my professor could not, and would not, sympathize with me. I expected him to meet me in my weakness and assure me that my deep, dark secret was safe with him. Now, I wasn't so sure.

Emotionally hurt and in so much physical pain, I packed my books into my bag. Thankfully, Krissy had waited for me. The whole building had gotten out of class at the same time and was making its way to the cafeteria. It would have been a nightmare to try to navigate the perilous halls with so many moving bodies in my line of sight unless someone walked with me and kept me from falling. For the semester, Krissy would become my partner in getting me to and from this class multiple times a week.

A few days later, I was in the middle of figuring out how to survive my first week of class in my compromised state, and I had to meet with the Dean of Students so he could check in on me.

We chatted a bit, and I told him that Meredith was in my class. He asked if we had talked, and I expressed my surprise that we hadn't.

He was surprised as well and suggested he set up a meeting with the two of us. He described what the meeting would be like and how he would, in essence, force her to apologize. I was confused and declined the offer. I did not want the Dean to force an apology. I wanted her to care about me, and I knew he couldn't make that happen.

I sat in the Dean's office many times during that semester, always hoping he was going to help me and always leaving feeling let down that he hadn't. It felt like our meetings were just for him to check off a box.

It was going to take everything I had to make it through the spring semester. One of the main reasons was because studying made me so tired. When I would try to study, I would fall asleep right where I was sitting. Quite frankly, I could fall asleep anywhere, at any time. This was unlike anything I had ever dealt with before. Friends would find me in the library sound asleep for who knows how long.

There were many reasons why I fell asleep, but it always came down to mental exhaustion due to intense concentration. Intense concentration was exciting and mentally stimulating before the accident. Now, *any* concentration was a burden, a hurdle that felt insurmountable as I tried to make sense of a simple math problem or even just a sentence someone said to me about their day.

Understandably, this made studying on my own a big hurdle and meant that I had to use my time exceptionally wisely. If I went on Instagram for just five minutes before beginning to study, my eyes would be seeing double, or I would just fall asleep.

I loved how quiet the library was. It was finally a place where I didn't have to be distracted by external noises that seemed to interrupt my thoughts. Before the accident, I constantly rewrote my notes or made flashcards to prepare for an exam. As a visual learner, seeing the information was the best way for me to retain it. Once I did that, it almost always stuck in my head.

Sitting in the library for my first study session of the semester brought back so much excitement to study and learn. I opened up the textbook and got out my new, clean notebook, writing the name of the class at the top.

I opened the assigned page and read the text, "Audit: to conduct an official financial examination…" I looked to my notebook to write the definition down and instantly forgot what I had read.

I read again, "Audit: to conduct an official financial examination…" Again, I instantaneously forgot the material as soon as I looked away from my textbook. I could not make the words stick in my head.

OK, this is hard. I thought. *Let's break it down more.*

I read and tried to retain the definition in parts, "Audit: to conduct an official…" In the time it took me to look from my book to my notebook, I had wholly lost the fragment of the definition.

I looked at the textbook and placed my left finger on the first paragraph. *Just write down "audit."* I highlighted the word in the book, thinking that could help me remember. My eyes moved from the word to my left, to the empty notebook on my right.

My mind was blank. An alarm went off in my head when I looked back to my textbook and saw the word highlighted in bright pink, jumping off the page as if to mock me as I put together the pieces of what was happening. Instead of feeling frightened or concerned, I began to get increasingly frustrated with myself. *What is wrong with you? Get it together! Try harder! WRITE. IT. DOWN.* I was furious and could not separate myself from my symptoms. Instead of feeling stupid, disgusting, and weak, I *was* those things. I was mortified to be trapped in my own body.

The more I focused on trying to do insurmountable tasks like this one, the more nauseous, dizzy, and overwhelmingly tired I became.

My memory issues manifested themselves in social situations too. I suppose this would've terrified me if I were aware it was happening. It was far more apparent to others than it was to me. Instead, I was in survivor mode. Each day was a considerable feat. Being a survivor meant living in the exact moment I was in, fixated on context clues and the facial expressions of others to maintain "normal" social interactions. It didn't matter if something felt confusing. Instinctively, I did whatever I could to regain control and awareness.

Every day I awoke with the dorm room spinning so quickly that I could barely get out of bed. I would go to the bathroom and throw up before most people would wake up, forming a quiet routine that wouldn't draw the attention of fellow sleeping students. I did not feel like constantly explaining to everyone why I was puking, especially because it became so commonplace to me now.

I was in way over my head but did not have the ability to admit it. I still could not pinpoint the triggers or the issues I was experiencing, so I kept to myself. There are not enough numbers in the world to count how many times I told myself to get over it and stop being such a loser. I truly believed I could be stronger than my symptoms if I just worked a little harder and pushed a little further.

On top of the physical symptoms, I was so emotional that I would break down hysterically sobbing somewhere on campus every day. I hated how weak that made me feel, but I also didn't know how to stop it. It seemed that everything had the power to lead me to tears, which was a huge departure from my emotional state before the accident. I didn't realize that the tears were my body's way of dealing with the stress I put on it. It didn't even occur to me that simply going to class and back to my dorm could be taxing on my body.

Sometimes I was genuinely sad because I was in so much pain, and sometimes it was just because I was past the point of extreme exhaustion like an overtired toddler ready for a nap. I was very fragile and tried to hide a lot of what was going on from people who had the power to send me home from school. School equaled worth, identity, and love in my mind. I told myself being sent home equaled weakness, worthlessness, unworthiness of love, and ultimate defeat. It was my body against my worth as a person, and I was drowning.

Around that time, while I was back at school feeling alone and awful, the chilling story of a girl from my county committing suicide hit the nation. It was the same raw winter air we both felt at our colleges just hours apart. She hadn't had an accident, so we weren't in the same situations, but I imagined I knew exactly how she felt. I imagined if I had to be sent home from school for how poorly I was doing, I could get *that* low. But for now, that mindset seemed tragically short-sighted for me, because I thought I would get better, although I *was* inexplicably sad. To cope, I rested in the hope that I would recover, and that God would use my pain. Philippians 4:13 (NKJV) rang in my ears: "I can do all things through Christ who gives me strength." To me, this meant I could get through the semester.

There were times I let my guard down to seriously question what was going on and examine the stress I was putting on my body. *Could I really be OK when I am throwing up all the time? Was this whole decision to be at school only based on my willpower alone?* In these times of reassessment, being sent home was no longer the enemy. I was looking forward to talking to my neurologist to seriously consider if I was actually OK. I wanted the truth, but the only symptom I could perceive well enough to describe was my constant nausea.

"I know throwing up right after an accident is terrible for some reason, but is it OK if I am throwing up every day because I am just so nauseated all of the time?" I held the phone to my ear, hoping for clarity or even a clue that could lead me toward a solution.

My neurologist cleared his throat on the other end and simply responded, "Throwing up now is a much different issue and not the same concern as throwing up right after an injury. One of these days, you're going to wake up, and be better and this stuff will just go away." I felt like he was giving me a doctor's note, stating that I needed to will myself to be OK again. *Jenna, you need to stop being so dramatic all the time and stop throwing up!* I told myself. *He seems to think you are fine. He is the one with a medical degree, not you. If he says you are fine, I'm sure you are.*

Despite my confusion, I was relieved each time I talked to him on the phone. He did not seem to be concerned about my excessive dizziness or ever-present nausea. I put my guard back up and solidified once again I had to do better, to *be* better, all by myself. If the doctor said I was fine, I just needed to push through and make myself *be* fine.

My mind was as clouded as the London fog, and I didn't remember what I was like before the accident. I loved the reassurance of others when I grinned with my red-lipstick smile and told them I was OK. Indeed, I *looked* like I was doing well. This felt like reassurance that I was OK…or at least that I was going to be OK. If only I could have articulated the differences before and after the accident, I might have come closer to understanding the serious neurological issues at hand.

In high school, I loved to tutor people in math. It was one of my great joys to be able to explain complex problems in easy ways. Now, just six months removed, tutoring felt more like torture than a source of joy. I was no longer the tutor, and I desperately needed help for the first time in my life. I needed to work with others because I could not complete my coursework on my own. So I went to every accounting tutoring night, which was held on Mondays, Wednesdays, and Sundays. I had to counter feeling stupid with still being able to complete my classwork well, and I was willing to do whatever it would take to succeed. If I tried to complete the homework by myself, I would fall asleep. When I was sitting in a room full of five people doing the work together, I could get by.

Weeks had gone by and I got to know the tutors fairly well. Most sessions went the same way: I would finish my first homework problem feeling confident I had completed each step correctly, but then when I compared my result with the other students being tutored, our numbers were completely different. I did my best to focus my eyes back through each step of the problem, but I couldn't discern what I had done incorrectly. The tutor would check over my problem and quickly say to me things like, "Jenna, you switched $15.70 to $5.70 three steps before the final answer!" Feeling defeated after each time this happened, I would correct my work with the help of a friend.

About a third of the way into the semester, one tutoring session in particular became the best example I'd use to explain my symptoms to the many doctors I visited later. I was looking at one textbook page for at least ten minutes and became totally exhausted. The room was spinning, but I was doing everything I could to concentrate and read correctly. The more I concentrated, the more I could feel dinner creeping back up my throat.

I was so frustrated. I thought I understood the material in that chapter, and I clung to it the best I could between my mental resets, but I did not have enough information to get the answer. The other girls in the tutoring session were all on the same textbook page as me, but I couldn't figure out where they were finding their numbers. I did not want to embarrass myself, so I looked and looked at every detail on that page for what felt like forever. Finally, I loudly exclaimed to the tutor in exasperation, "Grant, where are you getting the information from?"

He frowned. "What do you mean?" The girls looked equally confused at my exclamation.

"Where are those numbers? How did you calculate them? We are supposed to be looking in the textbook, right? I can't find them anywhere; what steps am I missing?"

"Jenna," he said calmly and with concern, "it's right in the chart."

"WHAT CHART?!" I cried in vexation. "There is *no* chart! Did the professor give us a chart?! Where is it? Why don't I have it? I have been looking at this page for ten minutes, and it turns out there is a chart I never got? How did I miss the extra chart handout?"

Grant walked over to me with a confused look and pointed about halfway down the page I had been looking at.

My eyes widened. I hadn't even seen the chart on the textbook page. It wasn't that I had simply overlooked the chart; I honestly hadn't seen it at all. It was no longer rare for me to miss small things like letters and numbers, but I had no idea I could miss large portions of my visual field such as a whole, half-page chart.

I was so embarrassed. I was so confused. I felt like a loser. My exclamation made no sense. Why did I freak out? I tried not to imagine what they must be thinking about me. I became very silent and hoped no one would ask me about the situation that had just unfolded. In an attempt to retain some dignity, I wrote down the answers for the homework and walked out. I did not want to talk to anyone or have to process what just happened and what was going on in my mind. I had used up all of my studying time for the day, so I needed to go back to bed.

Chapter 6

WHO AM I NOW?

was tired. I was sad. I was heartbroken. I missed my team. I was spending so much time trying to get back the life and goals I had before the accident that I didn't see how far from that reality I truly was.

The cold depths of winter were beginning to thaw, which meant it was almost time for spring tennis. I was making my way to the cafeteria and fell down. Again. I waited to stand up until the room stopped spinning so violently and smoothed to a rocking I could manage. This time, trying to make sense of the confusion sent my stomach into horrible flip-flops, and I ran to the bathroom uncontrollably gagging and vomiting. I started to cry. How could I still feel so horrible? Never in my wildest dreams did I consider that the symptoms would last this long.

I headed back toward the cafeteria because I knew I had to go eat. The uncertainty of whether or not eating would lead to another vomiting session took all of the enjoyment out of food, almost rendering it pointless. But in my weakened state, I convinced myself that not eating because I had an upset stomach would be immature. I knew my body needed food, so I forced myself through the cafeteria doors.

Through tearful, clouded eyes, I saw my tennis team walk in. They seemed to move in slow motion as their hair, perfectly brushed, glowed in the sunlight while they laughed back and forth with each other. I saw a mirage of my former self laughing with them. It was like seeing a long lost, unrequited love. It felt like my heart was being ripped apart.

Rushing through a river with an unexpected waterfall, I was sent over the edge crashing hard in the pool below. I began to weep, heaving and losing my breath uncontrollably. Not wanting to make a scene, I rushed out of the cafeteria and found myself a place to sit away from the crowd in a corner in the hallway that no one would see me in.

The girls all had their new warm-up uniforms on. I hadn't even been asked to be fitted for mine. Because our school was small and didn't have sororities or fraternities, our Division III sports teams were a huge part of campus life and a status symbol. I felt exposed and naked without the Nike logo they all sported. Who was I without the "Women's Tennis" label across my chest?

I was seeing for the first time that the team didn't need me. They had moved on, and I couldn't take it. I knew I would eventually be better and make it back to them. But for now, I was too weak for them, and that part of my identity was a gaping hole that I didn't know how to fill. They came into the building laughing and having a great time. I wanted to go with them to practice or even just to the gym, but the reality was I couldn't even walk to the courts a mile away and watch the ball go back and forth without severe symptoms.

I called my mom in this uncontrolled state. I was gasping for breath trying to tell her about the uniforms. They looked so good, and the girls were having so much fun. They were such nice girls, and I wanted to be a part of it so badly. Would I be on the team later this semester, or would I have to wait until next year? Who would I be until then? I wanted to put the work in. I wanted the friendships. I wanted them to need me. I wanted to be a family with them. More than anything, I wanted my identity back.

My mom calmed me down with comforting words, but I knew she was really worried about me. I did not want to have to go home and be even further from the goals I wanted to reach, so I put on something close to a smile and told her I was alright. I was sorry for losing it like I had.

I walked back into the cafeteria and sat with a few friends. My roommate wasn't there nor were my two closest friends, but these girls were friends who lived in my hall. They knew me and I knew them, although they weren't fully up to date on what life was like for me. I decided to give up the facade that I was OK and for the first time began to open up about the part of my life I was most ashamed of. This made me far more vulnerable than I was comfortable with, but hiding how I was truly feeling was not working very well either. Hopefully, they would try to understand and say something comforting.

"I don't know what's wrong with me…I can't read…I mean sometimes I can read a little…but after a few sentences I can't anymore." I held onto my words as long as I could, with long breaths between phrases, because it didn't make sense to me, and possibly wouldn't make sense to them either.

"What do you mean you can't read? You're in college! You can obviously read." The girl eating salad across the table quickly replied, missing my point completely. Although, I wasn't sure what my point was either.

"I know I'm in college." I blurted out abruptly and glared at her. The way she was eating her salad suddenly became a point of annoyance. Everything that moved seemed to trigger me. Each person's fork going into their mouth, each person walking by, each sight, noise, and smell was bombarding me, and I wished it would all be quiet and stop.

Sometimes I felt like everyone was right: it didn't make any sense.

Why could I sort-of read a few sentences sometimes and at other times I couldn't read at all? Why could I pose and smile in an Instagram picture and moments later collapse into bed? Why could I remember some things, but not others?

I realized I would have to do better if I was going to level with them. I had to figure out how to explain myself more clearly.

I desperately tried to think of even one example that would help describe my life. I dug and dug as for lost treasure into the depths of my unyielding mind.

"I can't remember things right. I try to...but I lose myself in the sentences...sometimes while they're happening. I'm just so..."

While I concentrated, crinkling my nose and closing my eyes, my friends stared back, waiting for me to finish my sentence. Feeling the pressure, I settled. "Confused. I'm just so confused." I breathed out and sat back in my chair, knowing that "confused" didn't even begin to describe my experience, but it was the most accurate word I could find. To be honest, I was thrilled I had found any word.

Looking around the table, I hoped to see faces that reflected under-standing and concern—but not too much concern because I also wanted reassurance that I was OK. I hoped that what I said wasn't too much or too unbelievable. I hoped it didn't sound too weird or too strange. For the first time, I had been genuine, speaking freely of how I really felt instead of covering everything with red lipstick and a smile.

I tried to decipher their expressions while I held my breath, anx-iously awaiting their response, expecting that someone would say something—anything really that would bring me comfort. Then Sarah, seated two chairs over from me, responded with the unimaginable.

"Oh, Jenna! I don't know why you are so sad! Everyone loves Dory!"

I thought for a second. *Dory? Who is Dory? The cartoon fish? What was wrong with her, again?*

"Oh, my gosh. Her memory," I whispered as I sat back in shock and horror.

Short-term memory loss, I thought to myself.

The rest of the table had broken into quiet laughter, thankful that someone had ended the awkward silence.

I sat there in utter disbelief.

Even though *I* frequently diffused embarrassing or awkward situations with humor—including the immediate aftermath of my accident—seeing other people make light of something I was so insecure about hit me like a ton of bricks. While so many of my friends had been so helpful and gracious, this comment seemed to cancel all of that out in one surreal, terrifying moment.

My identity as a serious student-athlete had eroded into a forgetful, fictional character. I don't think she could have said anything worse.

I knew I was having some memory issues but never understood that *that* was what the resets were. The comparison with Dory (though cruel to me) made my symptoms suddenly make sense, adding to the wave of shock and horror.

I couldn't breathe at the realization. I felt like I was deep in the depths of the ocean like in the movie, except I would rather drown as my old self than live underwater as Dory.

Similar to this moment with my friends in the cafeteria, Dory's memory loss was often portrayed as a punchline. I was not about to be a punchline. I was at this school on academic scholarship. I was a serious athlete. Did people think this horrifying thing I was dealing with was funny? I remembered how Dory could not get where she needed to go alone. She lived a life indebted to and dependent on others. She was always lost, and she was not in control of her life. I did not want to be lost. I did not want to be pitied and constantly out of control. I knew where I wanted to go in life, and I wanted to get there on my own.

The heartbreaking irony was, I was going to need help just to get from the table back to my bed.

These were dark days. I couldn't control my emotions, I couldn't control my body, I couldn't control my short-term memory, and because my double vision was so bad, most days I couldn't even find comfort by reading my Bible. Matt would call me every night and my mom every morning. They would patiently and gently listen to me, but their words alone could not counter my peers' inability to understand my situation, or the self-criticism in my heart. I desperately needed God to speak into my life.

One night, Matt was woken up by a fire alarm in his dorm that overlooked the Hudson River and New York City. He got himself outside into the freezing, 3:00 a.m. air and waited until he could get back to bed.

When he got back to his room, now wide awake, he couldn't shake the idea that he should leave a voicemail on my phone with that day's entry from a book of devotions we both liked. He dialed my number and opened the devotional to that day's date, not knowing what it would say.

That morning, I woke to the voicemail from Matt and a deeper message from God.

The devotion he read talked about not being discouraged when obstacles came our way. It talked about God's sovereignty and that we can't control the timing of our lives because God is sovereign and we aren't. It talked about living life moment by moment. Instead of rushing toward the goals we have created, we must live life outside the mode of ceaseless planning and trust God to provide what we need each moment.

I was so touched.

I picked myself up and wiped away my early morning tears.

"God, I give you this time in my life. It's so hard. I give you this week. I mean this day. I mean, I give you this moment. Help me to live life with you moment by moment."

The message on my voicemail meant so much to me that Matt recorded about three months' worth of devotions and some passages from the book of Psalms, my favorite book of the Bible, so I could listen to them on my phone. I continued to be touched by the words of God through those recordings, and the jokes Matt wrapped into the devotions never ceased to make me laugh.

Moment by moment.

Those words would become the backbone of my walk with God, a scaffolding on which I would stand to begin building my true worth and identity in Him again.

Underneath the surface I cried for help,
Desperately I pleaded as I fought the waves which took me away…

Chapter 7

HOW CAN I FORGIVE HER?

barely remember life without a GPS in our cars, and it sometimes baffles me how we used to get where we needed to go before them. I love the security of being able to hop in my car and be told right where to go. While driving, I don't have to fear that I am going in the wrong direction or if I will be late, because it continuously updates me with my next turn and time of arrival.

The peace and security of having a GPS suddenly vanishes when the dreaded "rerouting" symbol pops up. Did I take a wrong turn? Am I in a dead zone? All control is lost.

This is exactly how I felt, except my "rerouting" period had been going on for months.

One of the areas of my life in which I was being rerouted was how I saw Meredith. Week after week went by in that freshman class I shared with her, and she never so much as acknowledged me. Most classes, I had to leave in the middle of the lecture to throw up because I had been trying so hard to concentrate. Group work was after the lecture and always started with the members of the group going around and reading aloud a paragraph from a handout as part of class participation. The problem was, I was so tired and strained by the time group work started that reading was out of the question. I was the only one who was allowed to pass on reading the paragraph, as per my accommodations, which also meant I would have to explain my situation to each group I was a part of. I would bashfully explain I needed to skip because I had a bad accident during the previous semester and could not read. Inevitably, I would be asked how it happened, and I would tell them "the Glow Light Party," and everyone would remember. It was a story that almost every single person on campus knew about. I dreaded this even more than swallowing my own stomach acids as they would creep up my throat. I was humiliated that my inability to read was my reality, and I hated the attention. The last thing I wanted to do was tell anyone about it, but I couldn't fake reading something I had never read. Sometimes Meredith was in the group and sometimes she was not, but any doubts about whether or not she knew I was the person she hit with the cooler were erased by mid-semester.

One day, I sat in a group with her, and I asked someone sheepishly and quietly to read my paragraph for me. I realized that Meredith didn't look ashamed, she didn't look angry, and she didn't look sad. I had the stomach-churning thought that she was happy I was in such pain. But as more time passed, I came to realize she simply did not care what happened to me, good or bad. It was becoming clear that she could not be the enemy of my story. In order for her to be my enemy, she would have to care enough to hate me. If she was sorry, she already would have been forgiven by me. But she didn't care at all, and somehow her indifference was harder to accept than if she hated me.

I had dealt with forgiveness in the past, but this time was different.

I thought all the way back to middle school. One afternoon, all of my friends went around the room and told me they didn't want to be my friend anymore, each citing specific reasons and pointing out my flaws. Nothing was off-limits. Blindsided, I spent weeks not being able to see them without my stomach tying up into knots. Then God walked me through forgiveness of people who still disliked me. To my dismay, there was no reconciliation, but God was showing me how to let go of the pain and resentment I had begun to associate with my former friends.

I had also dealt with forgiveness when people had wronged me but were intensely sorry. Those situations are painful, but there is also a sort of transactional, expected way for the relationship to play out. There is a clear victim and a clear wrongdoer. The individual in the wrong feels contrite, which can make it easier to forgive. The victim who was hurt can decide to forgive and move on in the face of that emotion.

But for someone to completely derail my life and look at me with utter apathy toward both their actions and my well-being? I had never encountered something like that, and it threw off all of my preconceived notions of how forgiveness was supposed to go. I hated being rerouted in this manner because it meant even more confusion. Meredith's complete disregard for me caused me to lose even more control.

Each class, she just watched me suffer. She watched me leave to puke my guts out and then come back to try to make it through until the end. She watched my pain—pain she caused—and she did nothing to make it right or own up to her actions.

To make matters worse, a third of the entire coursework of that class was all about reconciliation and what the Bible has to say about it. We talked about how every hurtful situation in which we find ourselves calls for reconciliation. We talked about wrongdoing and forgiveness and even watched gut-wrenching videos of the Amish extending forgiveness to those who had murdered their loved ones.

I sat in the back of the room as the perpetrators in the videos came to the victims, torn up inside over what they had done. The videos showed the pain on both sides of the story. The perpetrators were guilt-ridden, and the Amish would forgive like it was nothing. It seemed right to me. I understood forgiveness. I understood its importance. What I did not understand was what forgiveness looked like when the person ruined your life, stripped you of your identity and your self-worth, and then took the last bit of power from you by making you see how little they cared about you (three times a week in class).

Midway through the semester, I got a text of a screenshot from one of my friends. Meredith had posted a "throwback" post on her social media of her and a friend from the Glow Light Party with a caption that said something to the effect of, "That was the best night of fall semester!" I could not be any more convinced that she simply did not care.

One day after I had left class to throw up, I sat on a couch in the hallway for about twenty minutes with tears running down my face. Life was so hard. My body rarely did what I asked it to do. It kept giving out. I had no control over anything anymore. I couldn't control my mind or my body, and I couldn't even get acknowledgement from the person who caused all of this pain. I wanted it to all be over. Alone, I went on my way back to my room, and my heart started to soften to how God was rerouting me.

"God, forgiveness is a decision, and I need you to guide me through this process." I could not control how she felt toward me, but I could control who I was putting in charge of handling the situation. I had to surrender complete control to God.

At that moment, my mom sent me a new Christian song she had heard on the radio. Its words, "Just be held," were precious to me. I cried and imagined God holding me.

God showed me that at the end of the day, forgiveness wasn't really between me and Meredith; it was between me and God. I had to release Meredith from the debt I believed that she owed me and that I was holding on to. I realized Meredith might never hold up her end of the forgiveness transaction, and she didn't need to in order for me to forgive.

Keeping a white-knuckle grip on my disappointment, sadness,

and feelings of being victimized by her actions made me feel like I still had a semblance of control in a wildly out-of-control situation. But I knew I needed to let even that go. The irony was that in living this way, I wasn't controlling her, *she* was controlling *me*. Hanging on to this hurt was only hurting me, and I needed to give it to God.

I needed to let go of my hurt for my sake. And in a time when I felt weaker and more helpless than ever, surrendering that pain to Christ allowed me to exchange my weakness for God's strength.

God was asking me a deep question: "Don't you know I am the one who sits on the judgment seat?"

For me, forgiveness is an example of ultimate trust in God and His plans for us. He is the judge, not me. We are to model our lives after Jesus who, while dying on the cross, said, "Father, forgive them, for they do not know what they are doing" (Luke 23:34). No one was showing remorse, no one was asking for His forgiveness, but Jesus freely surrendered the right to hold on to anger and bitterness. I knew it would probably always be painful and confusing to look back at how she treated me, but I was going to forgive her nonetheless.

Selfishly, releasing a person or situation to Christ through forgiveness is the best feeling ever. But in the moment, it seems like the most unselfish thing in the world. This is because you are turning what you think their punishment should be, over to God who will forgive her if she asks Him.

I knew I wanted perfect peace with Meredith rather than the pains of hatred, and I engaged God in the whole process constantly. Forgiveness was not an option for me but rather a way of living, as God had instilled it in me throughout my entire life. She owed a debt to me, and I was to release her of that debt. Why? Because I owed a debt to God, and He forgave me of that debt and came into my heart. It is the crux of the Christian faith. God reaches out His loving hand to us as we ask for forgiveness and understand the debt of our sin. He forgives us and makes our hearts His dwelling place.

Forgiveness took a few detours from what I expected, but I rested knowing that God, even more than a GPS, knows the whole picture.

Sitting in the class with Meredith for the rest of the semester was not always easy, but I no longer needed anything from her for me to be OK. I no longer waited in limbo, wondering what she would do or say or what she was thinking. I finally experienced freedom from allowing her actions to control me.

That's not to say that the rest of the semester was easy for me. It wasn't in the slightest. After spring break, each week felt like it could push me over the edge. In January, I thought I would feel so much better by February. In February, I supposed all the pain would be gone by March, and in March, I began to experience deep, deep sadness that my pain had not ended. Most days seemed impossible. I wanted to go home, but I knew that would mean all of the work I had put in during the first part of the semester would be for nothing. Exhaustion was setting in so deeply that it was hard to move my legs. It was hard to move anything. Without my friends from the dorm, there was no way I would have been able to make it through at all. Each took a turn helping me in various ways. Some read assignments to me, some walked me to class, some threw my laundry in with theirs, and some prayed as they wiped my tear-stained face. They picked up the slack for me when I could hardly hold on to the rope.

I clung to God, I clung to my friends, I clung to the words of my mother, and I clung to Matt and the devotions he recorded for me.

After I had finally finished my last exam, I collapsed into my bed and waited for my parents to take me home. The word exhausted no longer did my condition justice; it was far, far more drastic than that. I did not talk much to anyone, which I later realized was because I was barely able to.

Slurring, stuttering, and stopping in the middle of a sentence, not knowing what I just said or what I was going to say, now happened so much more often. I had pushed my body far beyond what it could handle, and it was breaking down even more.

My friends helped me gather my things and brought them out for my dad to pack into our car. I had lost the mental capacity to organize or categorize, so my parents packed the large pile of random items I owned and we brought them out to the curb. The pile had visible trinkets, sweatshirts, pens, papers, and sticky notes all together with clothing stuffed into my laundry bag. My dad, being the master organizer, took each item and placed it into the back of his black truck. That pile was a picture of the current state of my mind: random disarray. My body wasn't doing much better, and my neck and back hurt too much to bend down and pick up even my smallest items. It was a miracle I could even walk to the car. My dad somehow fit everything in and we went on our way.

When I got home, I slowly walked myself up the stairs. I could not believe it. The semester was finally over. I did it. I accomplished the impossible. I was thrilled, although I knew the experience had weakened me more than I ever thought possible. It was a horrible feeling knowing that, unlike the neurologist had said, I did not "wake up and feel better"during the semester.

Even though getting through my spring classes was an incredible achievement given my physical health, I hated that it had been so hard for me in the first place. Regardless, that was twelve credits in the books. Those plus the college credits I earned in high school meant that I was, by the grace of God, a sophomore.

I walked into my room to a bouquet of balloons that Matt had sent to my house. It had been such a tough and emotional semester for all of us. My whole family felt tired and accomplished, though the latter would be short-lived.

I had come so far but I had no idea I still had so far to go. I didn't know how much of myself would disappear into the darkness.

Chapter 8

WILL THIS EVER END?

Before the accident, if I was home more than a few hours I would become restless and need to get out of the house. I would feel like I needed to do something productive, something useful. I would work out, go for a run, get some errands done, meet with friends, and find anything at all to do that would not involve sitting in the house. After the accident, I was trying my best to live moment by moment, but I felt like I needed to do something of value for me to have any value.

I called up my boss from a previous internship at the county office and asked if another internship position was available. He must have liked something about me from when I previously worked in the finance department because the internship was secured in seconds after one phone call.

Right from the start, it was impossible for me to hide my symptoms from the other employees no matter how hard I tried. Still, I told myself I needed to push through the pain because I needed that internship for my resume.

I thought if I smiled enough and could handle myself for an hour, I could coast the rest of the day, collapsing or sleeping when necessary. Unsurprisingly, this did not fly in an office that demanded the completion of a full schedule of tasks, not to mention things like the basic ability to read, which I barely had. They sent me to the nurse's office to "sleep it off" whenever I collapsed. After a while, they no longer called when I was late to see if I would be making it to work that day. By then, they hoped I was in bed for my own good and not on my way into the office. I could not escape the intense symptoms I was feeling. Even the simplest of tasks stood as glaring reminders that something was very wrong. As I would sit on the couch in our living room, my mind would reset. I would desperately search for context clues.

OK, I'm home, I thought to myself. *OK, mom is here. What day is it?*

"Hey, Mom! What day is it?" I asked as I shut my eyes and crinkled my nose to try and find any clues in my memory to answer the question myself.

"Um, well…what day do you think it is?" She asked with a concerned voice. To me, it sounded a bit condescending, even though I knew she didn't mean it that way.

"UGH! Not again!! Can't you just tell me what day it is?" I cried in exasperation.

"Well, let's think through it together. What did we do yesterday?"

For some reason, remembering what happened the day before was one of the hardest tasks for me. All I knew was how frustrating it was to struggle to recall things that seemed so simple to others.

"MOM! I don't know what we did yesterday!" I couldn't help but cry out in frustration. I had absolutely no idea what we had done together just moments ago, let alone *yesterday*.

"You really don't know?" My mom squinted her eyes in concern.

"I really don't know," I admitted in disappointment.

"It's Tuesday," she breathed out in defeat.

"OK...thanks."

By this point, my parents and I could no longer sit and wait, wondering if I would wake up and feel better, so we scheduled many doctor appointments, beginning with a sports medicine doctor who had done wonders for a friend of mine with multiple concussions from soccer. Both of my parents and I sat in the tiny waiting room until I was eventually called in. The doctor came in with his prideful, loud personality and immediately made some jokes. After I quickly described the situation, he matter-of-factly said I had to quit my job (that I wasn't going to anymore) and stop trying to do normal activities. Absolutely no tennis (which I hadn't even attempted). Absolutely nothing exerting myself except a stationary bike for no more than seven to ten minutes.

I hyperventilated. "What do you mean??"

Even though I knew full well that I was not currently going to the office or playing tennis or even thinking of going to the gym, his restrictions broke me. Being in charge of what I should or should not be doing was the way I was able to assert my personal adult-like freedom that was crumbling before my very eyes. I liked having the final say on how I felt and what I did. With the doctor having such a take-charge personality, it would be weeks before my parents would think it was a good idea for me to start activities again.

He prescribed a bunch of supplements and asked me to do a short online concussion screening as part of his evaluation. Within moments of starting the screening, I ran from my seat in front of the office's desktop computer to the nearest bathroom to vomit. His mood changed immediately. It became clear that we wouldn't be scheduling a follow-up appointment with this doctor. In a matter of minutes, he went from wanting to be the "quarterback" of my recovery to advising us to see someone more specialized. He said I wasn't dealing with "just" a concussion; I needed serious medical attention. I was appalled by the regulations that he was putting on my life, yet his plan was wildly advanced for my current situation.

We then made an appointment with a neuropsychologist who had experience working with very serious head injuries.

I was mortified that I had to go to a neuropsychologist, because I wanted to get better on my own. Something about throwing the word psychology into the mix made me think that others believed I was exaggerating my symptoms or that they were all in my head. This then made me think that I could fix this entire situation on my own. At the same time, I was also frightened she would expose my insecurities and even worse, play into them. I was guarded, but my goal was to be as honest as possible.

The doctor had white hair and was about ten years older than my parents. Her office was a new, brick building about twenty minutes from my house. My mother and I arrived early so we sat in the car and prayed. I was so nervous.

Ten minutes before my appointment, we began to walk up the three flights of stairs and then continued through the winding hallway to her office. There were a few older people in the waiting room, and I tried to hide my face to keep my identity a secret because I was so embarrassed I was there.

My name was called, and we went to the back office. There were two purple couches, and my mother and I took a seat on the larger couch. The room was bright with natural light which caused my ever-present light sensitivity to spike, bombarding my already tired eyes with more pain. The doctor smiled and started to ask us a few questions. She listened to us speak but had a concerned look on her face the entire time.

I could tell she saw through my smile. This frightened me. Most people did not see through my facade like that. She could tell things were terribly wrong. While I couldn't imagine how my symptoms were connected to a more serious, physical reality, she knew that they were. She also knew why different things were confusing for me, and why I had so much pain in specific areas. She kept a lot to herself that first visit, and we scheduled another visit for testing the following week.

The testing was so strange to me and very extensive. Some of the tasks were easy, and some were insurmountably difficult. She put a garbage can next to me in case I threw up and was very accommodating when I needed to stop testing to rest or recover from the room's constant revolutions. For some of the tests, I could work for only about five minutes at a time. I did not understand what the testing was going to accomplish, so I just tried to do my best.

Finally, we got her report. She sat my mother and I down. A cool breeze of nerves shivered down my spine, reminding me how much of my own value was at stake. I had no idea how to make sense of her puzzles and what the right answers were supposed to be, so I had no idea what she was going to say.

Though I had spent my time since the accident paralyzed by the fear that my new symptoms meant I was lazy and suddenly unintelligent, she made it clear that this was not an intelligence assessment.

For the first time, she was connecting specific symptoms with specific parts of my brain that were injured.

She began, "Do you know what a contusion is?"

My mother and I looked at each other, remembering from my MRI that I had two of them and shook our heads up and down. My mom replied, "Yes! Well, we looked it up of course, so yes, but no, not functionally…"

"A brain contusion is a bruise on the brain," the doctor explained. "Functionally, the injured part gets shut off and will not turn back on. You can find ways to re-learn things by using other parts of your brain, but the injured part will not come back. Now if you look at the testing, you can see which parts were shut off."

We looked at each other and then back at the doctor in unified bewilderment. I shifted in my seat and sat up a little straighter as if that would help me understand better. I started to digest what she said as the symptoms I felt started making more sense.

That was what my mind was desperately trying to do: relearn new ways of doing things to compensate for the damaged parts. It was all starting to make sense. Some things were fine, and other things I simply lost the entire ability to do. I was compensating and had no idea what to compensate for. It finally answered the question of why I could do some things without any problems and why other tasks would practically knock me out. She explained how serious it was and that all of the symptoms were due to the fact that my brain did not know how to do the things I was asking it to do anymore. One contusion would be bad. I had two.

She went on to explain that my IQ was high, but my processing was extremely low. She explained this disparity of IQ and processing is not possible without a terrible injury.

My overworked body hung on my bones. I was relieved she didn't question my intelligence, but I was overwhelmed with the prospect that it would take more than a couple weeks of rest from the semester to get me better.

After her full report, we were a bit stunned. It actually all made sense, but it was so bad. It was the first time I heard the title "traumatic brain injury." At first, I thought she was just describing me and what I was dealing with, not realizing it was an actual name of an injury. With this new diagnosis (and how much sense her assessment made), we were rather shocked at the way that the original neurologists handled my situation.

The neuropsychologist recommended multiple therapies (some I had never heard of), including vestibular, cognitive, vision, and physical therapy.

My mom scoured the internet and called hospitals, rehab centers, and the insurance company all day, every day. She had to figure out what the therapies were and where to go for them. Down the Garden State Parkway we went, with me as the copilot in the heat of the summer. With sweat running down our faces and hair sticking to our necks, we would get into the car a few times a week and go to different therapies. Generally, when traveling to a new place off the parkway, it would be helpful for the copilot to be able to read the map on our phones without double vision. But I couldn't help my mom with *anything, ever, at all.*

Like a nightmare on repeat, I still remember turning into the rehabilitation facility for the first time. We found a parking space in the busy lot filled with transportation cars for wheelchairs. We took a deep breath and looked at each other. I knew I had to go in. I winced from emotional pain as my physical body ached.

Walking into the facility was unlike anything I had ever experienced—the sights, the smells, the people. The whole building smelled like an unkept nursing home with the occasional scent of urine. I wanted to walk out the minute I walked in. Every single person I saw had sad, somber looks on their faces. Each was weighed down by a burden, like they were wearing a hundred-pound jacket. The weight of the burden turned their eyes to the ground, and it was as if each person begged you not to look at them.

To my right were the most wheelchairs I had ever seen in one place. Then, the elevator chimed to my left. I glanced over as the doors from the cognitive wing slowly opened. I could not help but stare. There before me stood a man with a walker, going about two inches per hour. He looked like he had been to outerspace, with bars connecting parts of his head to the huge, round, glass, fish-bowl helmet. I continued to stare, wondering about the reason for the helmet. Then, as he turned, I saw that a large part of his head was missing. This man, in his thirties, tall, with dark shaved hair and a scruffy beard, was leaving the same people that could hopefully help me. He walked in a diagonal line, attempting to go straight, and headed for a therapy room.

He had a traumatic brain injury. I had a traumatic brain injury. Staring at the man blankly with my mouth open for who knows how long, I was suddenly filled with the desire to never want to see him again. I froze in fear for a few moments, unable to move or process anything around me. I felt electrocuted by the shockwaves of my surroundings. I forgot how to walk and stood paralyzed. It took a few moments for my mom to grab my arm and continue forward to find the right room.

My throat welled up and I swallowed hard. Tears started streaming down my face, and I tried to be strong.

It was too much for me to handle. There was a fire burning in my stomach as harsh words spun around my mind toward this man. Did I hate this man? How could I possibly hate him? I didn't even know him! Still, I knew with every fiber in my being that I never wanted to see him again. Constantly forgetting my surroundings, I tried desperately to forget this man. Where had my compassion gone? I was stunned by my own reaction. I don't remember ever hating *anyone* much less someone I didn't know who was hurting as badly as he was. It took a few days for me to realize why I had these feelings toward him.

Walking into cognitive therapy meant that there was something wrong with my mind. It was the biggest blow to my pride I could have ever imagined. I had built up my mind my whole life. I imagined that you could take anything from me except my ability to learn, think, remember, and process. It was my security and my greatest asset. Mortified and humiliated would not even come close to describing how much I couldn't bear the idea of needing cognitive therapy. I despised the idea that I had to seek help for my mind to function properly. It was the last place in the world I wanted to be, even though I had full confidence it would "fix me."

The injured man represented a new path for my life that I didn't want any part of. The chunk taken out of his head reminded me that there was a chunk (however small) "taken out" of my brain, if what the neuropsychologist said was true. The gaping hole in his head exposed the gaping hole in my heart. This poor man, walking alone, was not inviting my comparison, but it flooded through me like a loud wave cracking over top of me. His physical appearance was now my reflection, and I felt disgusting, despicable, and a shadow of the person I could be. Just months before, I was hating myself to new levels because I could not go to the gym or anywhere other than my class and my dorm. Where I was now was ten times worse. I longed for a word even nastier than "hate" because I would've used it against myself every moment I walked those halls.

Despite the fog I was feeling as I tried to gather my thoughts, I needed to find my way to the correct waiting room.

I could barely breathe and could not stop shaking as I walked the halls and eventually sat down on the green and brown checkered couch. *You're OK*, I thought to myself hoping that would stop the shaking.

They called my name after some time, and my mother and I walked in and sat down with three cognitive, occupational therapists. We took a deep breath in the hot and stuffy room that looked like it had not been redone since 1970. The window AC unit blared in my ear, and we all sat, my mom and I resting our arms and legs cautiously in the sterile therapy room. The first woman to speak, who sat in the middle chair across the table, was very sweet but talked in a way that made me feel like I was five years old. She explained that there would be a long process to the therapy but that it would help me so much. To me, long sounded like a few weeks or a couple of months, and I knew I had that window of time before I needed to go back to school in the fall.

The first day was a cognitive evaluation so the therapists could write up a plan. I was nervous and wanted to do the absolute best that I could. I began the testing wanting to show that I was much better off than the other patients who had visible and severe disabilities. I wanted to demonstrate that I was very smart. I wanted to make it clear that *I* was not like the others who walked through these office doors.

My mindset that day was, of course, far from biblical. I never remembered ever looking down on others with disabilities or questioning their worth or value, but that was before I was a patient at a rehabilitation center. How I saw myself never seemed to affect how I saw those around me, especially those with severe disabilities. I wasn't sure why it was different now, as I scrambled to find reason for myself to feel worthy of love, in any form.

I sat in front of the therapists tall and poised. I tried to answer their questions with the most eloquence I could muster. I refused to be their "typical" cognitive therapy patient, as I heard adult voices screaming and arguing in the other therapy rooms. These were patients who were clearly not being able to make sense of themselves. Despite my pretense, I was screaming too, just on the inside.

"You said you are very dizzy. Have you ever fallen down?" The lead therapist asked.

"Oh yes," I replied. "Lots of times." I was happy to encourage her in my next words. "But it's OK, I have learned to fall on my bottom, so I don't get hurt. I've never gotten really hurt when I fall. Sometimes the ground is actually much better than standing because when everything feels like it is moving, I am sturdier when I am sitting or lying on the ground. Even when I am so tired that I collapse, I have never hurt myself badly."

"I see…" she said as she wrote things down on her paper. She checked boxes and made notes. "Do you cook at all?"

"Yes! I love to bake! It is one of my favorite things to do!" I glanced at my mother who looked at me squinting her eyes, knowing that she was not supposed to jump in and answer for me. I paused and gathered my thoughts. "Well, I mean, I don't bake anymore…"

"And why is that?" the therapist asked.

"Well I've tried, and it doesn't work. I can't do it anymore," I said looking down in embarrassment, as my cheeks began to flush.

"What do you mean it doesn't work?"

"Well, I never remember what ingredients I put in. I try to remember but then I get really tired and dizzy and have to stop. I find myself holding an ingredient and wondering if I have just put it in or not, and then it's just a big mess someone else has to clean up because I am asleep."

"You cannot remember the ingredients? Have you tried utilizing a checklist?"

"It all happens quicker than that," I said, trying my best to articulate the experience. "I put the ingredients in and by the time I grab the pen I don't know what I just put in the mixture. It's like it disappears. Then when I try to remember, the room spins and spins. I get so nauseous I puke, and then I'm so tired I fall asleep…but I am really good at baking!! Or at least I used to be… I… I… I… yeah…" My voice trailed off as my therapist began to write in her notebook.

"Do you live alone?" she continued.

"No, I live with my parents."

I was wondering why all of this was pertinent information for her to know until she began to explain to my mom that I should not attempt to bake and how big of a deal it would be if I left the stove on by accident because it could burn our house down.

I felt like a small child. Why wasn't she directing that comment to me? I understood the importance of turning off the stove! She was overlooking me as if I could not hear her. I was no longer an asset to my family. I was a liability. They needed to "watch" me. She talked about me as if I wasn't even there, making me think she saw me as so injured that I would not care about her insults. I was horrified with embarrassment.

I felt like a bug in the room swarming around and annoying everyone. One that everyone would rather see dead than alive.

With the initial patient questionnaire over, it was time to start the testing. The first test was to write down the number seven every time I heard it from a speaker. The catch was that they played two speakers, one with the numbers and the other with a muffled news broadcast. I took a deep breath. Seven. That's easy enough. I can remember seven. I wrote down the number on the blank page so I would not forget my task and looked down at the page to block out everything else in my peripheral vision.

Radio One: *muffled radio static*, "The weather today will be a mix of clouds and rain…," *muffled radio static*, "This week the New York Yankees won their second season game." *Muffled radio static.*

Radio Two, at the same time: "One…Five…Six…Seven…Two… Five…Nine…Four…Seven…Two…Zero….Two…Seven…"

The room went from gentle rocking to sudden spinning. I was absolutely incapable of blocking out the news broadcast to listen to the numbers. I think I wrote down only one or two sevens before it was all too much. I tried my hardest not to vomit, swallowing hard on the stomach acids, but not even a minute into the first test, I found myself getting up and sprinting down the hall toward the bathroom.

Leaning over the chipped, pink toilet, I wretched and puked uncontrollably with unrelenting dizziness. Hateful thoughts filled my mind. *Jenna, you are such a loser. Why could you not just write down the sevens? Come ON. Get it together. You can't even decipher between words and numbers without getting sick?*

I wiped away the tears on my face. I sighed and stiffened my body that I hated so very much in that moment, as if that would help me regain some control. I hated that it was so weak and that I felt so horrible. I stood up and rested myself against the cold, yellow, tiled wall, careful not to move my neck to prevent more dizziness. I was so glad I was away from all of the radio noise and people walking up and down the hallway. Every movement, every sound, every color, and every smell was *so* strong and apparent to me, even more so, it seemed, in this center. The largest thing in the room seemed just as important as the tiny details in my mind. I closed my eyes to escape it all for just a moment.

"Jesus, I need you," I whispered feebly with the small amount of strength I had left. "Please help me. Please heal me. I trust you. I want to get out of here. Please make it all stop." I knew I needed Him more than ever.

Suddenly, a loud, persistent knocking came at the door, startling me out of my prayer. It sounded as if whoever was there could push the entire door down.

"Jenna!" yelled my therapist. "Are you OK? Are you in there?"

Startled, I replied, "Uhh...Yes I am. I will be out in a minute." *Why had she followed me to the bathroom? Weird.*

"I need you to unlock this door *right now!*" she yelled sternly, which caught me off guard.

"Um, OK?" I guess I was going to have to explain that I threw up. I thought that would be obvious from exclaiming how nauseous I was, grabbing my stomach, and running to the bathroom. I also thought she would appreciate the fact that I went to the bathroom and did not choose to get sick on her office's shag carpet floor.

I worked my way over to the sink and washed my hands using the grimy faucet. Filling my cheeks with air, I let out a big breath and prepared myself to speak to this woman.

When I opened the door, the therapist was actually angry with me. She said I was not allowed to go anywhere in the building by myself in the allotted session time.

"What? I am fine. Why?" I said defensively.

"With the symptoms you have described, we are not allowed to let you travel anywhere by yourself in the building. Next time you feel sick, you simply need to explain yourself and I will accompany you to the bathroom."

"I'm sorry, you need to go to the bathroom with me?" I said, confused and agitated. I looked at her as if she had three heads, and with my double vision, she looked like she did.

Apparently, a statewide regulation applied to my situation which meant I would not be able to travel anywhere in the building alone during the session time, for liability reasons. I couldn't even throw up on my own anymore.

I was not as much insulted by her remarks as I was heartbroken. In the wide range of people in cognitive therapy, I was someone they were worried about. I was someone they saw as "very bad," so bad I had to be followed around. Perhaps she thought I would get to the bathroom, reset, and not know where I was. Perhaps she thought I would fall down and get hurt and it would be her fault because she let me out of her sight. I hated that the scenarios I thought of were actually realistic. They were worried for my safety and that of others by simply letting me out of their sight. There were adults with disabilities, all alone, loudly acting up within earshot, but they were worried about *me*.

After my sessions were completed that day, we went to leave the building. On our way out, there were countless amputees waiting patiently to be picked up by their rides. Most of the time, it seemed these people were all alone. A bus would come and pick up each person and bring them home.

I looked at my mom as we got in the car.

"I know," she said looking back as she gave me a reassuring nod. With that nod came an understanding that we weren't about to cry. It was almost too sad to cry.

"I'm so sorry…for everything…" my voice cracked as I murmured my apology.

"Stop," she said abruptly but with kindness in her eyes. "Don't be. We're going to get through it."

Driving me to therapy that summer was going to take up most of our days. There were countless things she had given up, friendships put on hold, and sacrifices she made in order to take care of me full time. She spent most days driving me around and most nights researching words on my MRI for doctors or therapies that could help.

"Thanks so much for being with me. I'm really thankful for you," I said feebly once we pulled out of the facility and our eyes had seen the last of the patients waiting for their caretakers to pick them up.

"Where else would I be?" She smiled and patted my arm before using both of her hands to turn onto the parkway.

I had so many unspoken thoughts that fragmented and diluted into the blankness of my mind. I knew that my greatest blessing was my family, but my biggest wish was that I could take all of the hurt upon myself instead of having to watch my injury hurt those I loved.

The Worst Part of It All…

The worst part of it all…
Was the not the pain she felt,
Or puke in the bathroom stall.

It was not the doctors' prognosis,
The events she missed,
Or symptoms that made her lifeless.

The worst part of it all…
Was the tears she heard from the other side of the wall…
It was the fact that it all had taken a toll.

That troubled look on her dad's face,
The sorrow in her mother's heart.
The agony she wished she could erase…

If only she could overcome.
The worst part of it all…
Was that she could not overcome

….without them.

The therapists gave me numerous packets to read that were supposed to help me manage my life around my injury. In the few moments I was able to read each day, I tried to decipher the new structures and routines the packets spelled out in agonizing detail. As I tried to put the techniques into practice, I realized it was actually making me more nauseous and fatigued to try to live in these oddly specific ways, counter to my personality. Weeks went by and I didn't get any better, using all of my mental and visual stamina reading small parts of these packets and sitting through meetings.

I have never in my life failed to complete a homework assignment, but I physically could not do the work they wanted me to, and I expressed that to them many times. They never called in my family for progress reports like they had suggested, and I never saw the head of the department after the first visit like they said I would. Nothing worked for me, which left me feeling even worse about myself. Living my worst nightmare at cognitive therapy felt like it would be worth it once it fixed me and I was restored to my normal self, but it didn't heal me. We had put so much hope into this rehabilitation but were met with another dead end.

The whole experience begged a few questions: Who *do* they help? How do people with cognitive or memory issues like mine find healing? How are we going to fix my issues if they can't?

It was more of the same story in the other therapy programs I was in. So much work and pain for so little progress, if any.

After weeks up and down the New Jersey parkway, my therapists one by one discharged me. Being discharged somehow felt worse than starting the programs. I didn't fit into their molds, and they couldn't fix me like I assumed they would have.

By the end of summer 2014, I found myself at the beach again, looking out at its vast expanse off the New Jersey shoreline. To my dismay, I was in no condition to go back to school or live on my own; that was obvious.

Taking in the salty air and feeling the winds of change, I knew what I had to do. I walked up to the house and called my friends to tell them I would not be able to come back to school that semester.

The call was filled with promises of returning to school for the spring semester and other promises I wouldn't be able to keep—imaginings of future fun, friendship, and life together. I told them I would once again be the version of myself we all loved, although I was far from her at the moment.

The exacerbation of therapy arguably had left me even worse than before. My hatred for what I had become sunk to new depths. As the fiery orange sun set on a long and painful summer, my vestibular system rocked me like I was being tossed by the waves. I braced myself for another round of new therapies, but remained ever so tired and confused about who I was. I had fought against the waves of injury and insecurity for months, but was beginning to lose the will to continue. The riptides pulled me under, and I couldn't breathe. I had no idea how much longer I would need to struggle against the ocean, and I worried that I was about to drown.

Chapter 9

ARE YOU DROWNING?

I bled through my bandages,
Leaving a trail wherever I went.
I thought by now I'd be healed,
But those wishes were as good as spent.

The seasons had drifted from summer to fall, but the season of my life remained constant.

We were about to travel into the city once again for something that seemed like it could be "the answer." We were going to a consultation at a rehabilitation center in New York with both inpatient and outpatient care, including an entire program just for people with head injuries and brain trauma. This program had an all-day, everyday option that my mom and I would have to attend together.

We found the program the same way we had found many of the other avenues we went down: my mother, google searching the words from my MRI scans to see who helps people with diagnoses like mine. She was relentless in researching possible avenues to guide and support me on the long and winding road of my recovery. She refused to give up hope. We had been praying and seeking, and I really thought this was going to be just what I needed.

Something about the crisp air of the beginning of fall and the beginning of a new program excited me. Perhaps the best program in the world (as it was touted) for cognitive function would be able to fix me. This program was very selective, with applications and interviews that reminded me of the college acceptance process.

I picked up my weak body and plopped myself into my dad's car as we readied ourselves for another drive to the city. Next to me, I kept a bag filled with ginger ale and Swedish fish, my new diet to combat car sickness.

After suffering through loud stop-and-go traffic, I walked out of the parking garage on the Upper East Side and steadied myself on the brick steps beside the garage. I felt tossed from side to side, and I was unable to see where the ground was. I started to vomit because of the extreme dizziness spurred on by the car ride into the city, but I held it back the best I could to avoid spurting vomit in front of the posh New Yorkers walking by.

I grabbed my dad's arm and we headed across the street toward the large building which housed the rehabilitation center. Halfway across, I wished I had thrown up already because there was no holding back at this point. The ever-approaching taxi cabs meant I could not stop in the middle of the street, so I raced into the building to find the bathroom.

After I was done, I gathered myself together, reapplied my lipstick, and took a deep breath.

We made our way to the sign-in counter and walked into the waiting area. The program doctors invited us in and said it was such a perfect day for us to visit. It was the ending of their previous session cycle, and each patient would be sharing about their experience. We sat down, not sure what to expect. Each patient was with their main caretaker, usually their spouse or parent. It was not always easy to tell who the patient and who was the caretaker were, at least until the patient got up to share.

One after another, each patient went carefully through their planned speech. Some had an easier time than others, but each speech was filled with pauses and obvious difficulties.

A few patients had slurred speech, while others had lots of breaks in their thoughts. Some could barely speak at all. Some had obvious physical challenges while others appeared fine. It was shocking to see and hear testimonies of people with severe mental disabilities and realize I could be a part of their group. Was I really that bad? My MRI and recent diagnoses said so, but that didn't make this experience less shocking. I squirmed in my seat, embarrassed for my fellow accident victims. I could not imagine sharing with others how poorly I was doing, and each one continued to do so. It was clear that all of these patients still had serious processing challenges, even at the end of the long program. Rather than testimonies of radical recovery, the graduates detailed how they would never be the same after their accident, but that they were in a much better place emotionally and felt more equipped to live after the program.

My squirming turned to paralyzing fear with each testimony. When were the testimonies of how the program fixed people going to start? When were they going to talk about how they can go back to work? Some were lawyers, doctors, or businessmen. None of them were functioning well enough to work at the levels they used to. They were all in a better place to live life, but it was not their old life. Some read the popular poem called "Footprints." In this poem, a person walks along the shore and sees two sets of footprints in the sand, but after a while, he sees only one set. He thinks, *God, why have you abandoned me?* But then he realizes there is only one set of footprints when times get tough because it is God carrying him. Some talked about how grateful they were to be alive. Some could barely talk at all.

Hearing their stories, I was completely frozen in fear, disappointment, and overall shock.

Following the testimonies, my parents and I were approached by one of the neurologists. "Would you guys like to follow me?" she asked with a big smile.

We obliged and were then ushered into a room with about four doctors who specialized in cognitive neurology. They told us more about the program and asked me my interview questions.

"So Jenna, tell us about your accident," the first doctor said with regal poise.

"Um, well…hi, my name is Jenna Shotmeyer. I'm 19 years old." I went on to explain what I knew about what happened to me and fragmented pieces of what my days were like.

"Yes, we have seen some of your testing results and your MRI scans," the second doctor shared after I had done my best with the story. "Now, Mr. and Mrs. Shotmeyer, I am not sure if you are aware of the healing window of traumatic brain injuries. There is about a six-month to one-year window that people with injuries like your daughter's heal. After that, the window is closed." He was repeating a common theme we had started hearing from other doctors and hospitals.

A doctor who had not spoken yet turned to us and said, "Jenna is going to have to learn a new way of doing things, and that's where we come in."

"Do you think your program is going to help her?" my mom asked.

"Oh, why yes. Jenna is the perfect candidate. Although I must tell you that people diagnosed with a TBI only ever get back at most 80% of what they used to be able to do. In your daughter's case, the healing window is now closing so we cannot promise such a high percentage. Just like the people we saw earlier who shared their stories, we want to help Jenna find a path to a better place, not go back to who she was." The first doctor reassured us with a smile as if he had said something encouraging.

They accepted me, but I rejected everything about them.

I was taken aback that they thought I was such a great fit for their program, because they dealt with people who had serious, life-altering injuries. I was just a college kid, and I didn't want to be wrapped up in a tragic story; I just wanted my life back.

There was a huge difference between me and the people in the program: they had lost who they used to be, but I absolutely had to get back to who I used to be. If I couldn't be who I used to be, I didn't want to be here at all. I refused to accept my new limitations.

I hated hearing the doctors say my "window of healing" was closing after a whole year had passed. *This* is who I would be forever? This pathetic shadow of a person was what I had to deal with now?

I wanted to scream but my breath was taken away. The eerie truth of the complexity of my injury crept in shivers up my spine as I had now been correctly diagnosed by about ten doctors, all touted as top in their field, and they all told us my chances of getting even a bit better were extremely low.

In a flash, my weakly-constructed denial collapsed before my eyes. All of my symptoms were related to a physical injury of my brain: the resets, the vision problems, the nausea, everything. I thought I knew myself best, but in a moment, I realized I was a complete stranger to myself now. It was all coming together, and I couldn't take it.

Before the accident, I was dissatisfied with myself and strived to be the person I thought I was going to become. Now, after this several-hour meeting, I had hit a brick wall. I could no longer become my ideal future self, nor could I return to the person I was before the accident—a version I was already dissatisfied with. I couldn't breathe as I realized this person I was now, the one I hated more than ever, was who I could forever be. There was no chance I could love this version of myself, and I didn't even want to try. I couldn't figure out a reason for me to stay on earth if I had no worth to anyone. I was no longer a student, an athlete, or a friend. I could not think of any label to describe myself. I had no more value or identity. I had failed completely. I failed God. I failed myself. I failed everyone around me.

The culmination of these thoughts and feelings all came together in the cold hospital room as I was being accepted into the world-renown rehab program that wouldn't even attempt to fix me.

It was the worst day of my life.

For the first time, I was forced to admit to myself that everything I had built was gone. All my life's work—gone.

Perhaps I would be worthless forever.

Interestingly, I didn't think the people in the program were worthless. The thoughts that spiraled about the man with the missing piece of his skull had been different than what I thought about these new people. I hadn't heard the story of that man; I only saw what he looked like. After hearing the stories of the people at this program, I thought they were courageous. The stories made me have compassion and added a human element to the scene. It took a lot for them to get up there and say the things they did. I had compassion for them but somehow none for myself.

They were victims of horrific accidents and were working out what their new life was going to look like. But while I saw their courage in the face of hardship, I was still completely unwilling to come to terms with this new life for myself. What seemed like a good plan for them was vastly different from what I thought was a good plan for me. While I admired them for their hard work to rebuild their lives, when applied to me and my life, it felt like quitting and succumbing to a lesser version of myself. I didn't want to be like them.

We drove out of the city, back to the suburbs just in time for sunset. I grabbed my camera and walked from the house down to the lake I lived on. I sat in the dirt paying no mind to my pants that would inevitably stain. I marveled at the surface tension of a leaf on the water as the night fell from dusk to darkness.

"Sometimes the greatest feat of all is keeping your head above the surface," I wrote on my Instagram with a picture of the leaf just barely suspended on the water.

I felt like I was slowly drowning in the black water of night, floating just enough to stay alive. Thoughts weaved in and out of my mind. Perhaps I would never be needed again.

I wanted to be in school. I wanted freedom. I wanted to be studying. I wanted to be able to go for a run. But what I wanted didn't seem to matter anymore. How frustrating it was that all of my former coping mechanisms, hobbies, and activities were now things I was physically unable to do.

In addition to my disappointment in myself, I proved to be a disappointment wherever I went. My high school athletic director, who had proudly hung up the newspaper clipping of my first college win on our high school bulletin board, teared up when my parents told him how I was doing. Mothers and fathers of friends would break down and cry or get horrifyingly angry at my school and the girl who threw the cooler. Telling my parents' friends at church how badly I was doing was somehow even worse than all of the lights, sounds, and symptom-triggers of being in the building. One man who had known me my whole life sobbed on my shoulder during a prolonged hug because now, a year after the accident, he was still devastated by what happened to me. I always loved to be the one encouraging others, but now my life story brought everyone down.

I couldn't face my grandparents who were shattered by what happened to their granddaughter. They wanted the old Jenna back and so did I. It broke them, and all I could do was watch. I had never heard a grown man cry like my grandpa did as he sobbed on the phone after I shared with him how my life was going. I knew it was because he loved me, but I could not get over the fact that I made him so sad when I used to make him so happy. To make matters worse, I thought I had been so positive, intentionally leaving out certain heartbreaking details.

It was never my intent to make grown men cry and leave women who loved me discouraged. I often found myself consoling friends and family who were sad *for* me. People began to say things like, "That is the worst story I have ever heard. You are so strong to be able to handle it." I knew full well it could not possibly be the worst story they had ever heard, but they really seemed to mean it. And how could they say I was strong when I hated every part of every day?

"It's OK, I'm OK," I said, not knowing what else to say to people.

"It's NOT OK!" shouted my former tennis instructor who had worked countless hours with me to prepare me for my college team.

"Yeah, I know…"

Much more than being a perfectionist, I was a people pleaser. Perhaps I was a perfectionist at being a people pleaser, burdened when anyone around me was unhappy. I lived my whole life for others' approval and happiness, so the sadness around me broke me.

I had let down a whole community, a community who had given me so much love. They were so proud of me as I went off to school, and I hadn't kept up my end of the bargain.

My lack of ability let down my former educators who poured so much into my life. They had given glowing recommendations to the colleges I applied to, and I could no longer back up what they said about me. So many people mentored me to make the best version of myself I could be, and it was all for nothing.

I had let down our church body who had prayed for me and poured into my life so I could go out into the world and share Jesus. But I could barely go anywhere except to the doctors. Who could I share Jesus with while I was alone in my bed?

It didn't even occur to me that God could accept me as I was. I had made everyone around me sad and disappointed, so I figured God must be sad and disappointed with me too. It didn't make sense to me that God could think of me as anything else but worthless to Him. My identity for a long time had been in what I thought I could do for God; now that I was hardly able to do anything and had no vision for what I would be able to become, all I had left was the label "worthless."

I was crippled by the idea that God used to have a plan for my life, and I had lost it. I had failed Him. I had failed my family. I had failed myself. I used to have a mission field. I was a conqueror. I was an overcomer.

I was weighing down my family. I was weighing down my boyfriend. I was literally dead weight because to me all the good parts were gone.

The most chilling piece of this whole experience is that this was not all in my head. My warped mindset came, in part, from reality. I was disappointing people. I had let people down. People cried everywhere I went.

Before the accident, I believed I was my worst critic, but when everything fell apart, I realized that some other people were far more critical of me than I ever was. I overheard a conversation of a friend telling another friend they should not tell a certain boy how bad the accident had left me because if Matt broke up with me and this boy and his friends knew how bad I was, none of them would ever date me.

The comment made me feel even more nauseous than usual, not because I was particularly worried about my relationship with Matt or my prospects of future relationships with others, but because I believed the premise behind what she said. I would never be enough. Once you compared me to someone else, anyone else, I wouldn't measure up.

I couldn't shake the notion that the world would be better off without me. My family and boyfriend were so upset by what happened to me; what would it matter if I wasn't here anymore? As time passed, their unconditional love for me, which I didn't understand, felt more and more like a burden. They were already so sad. They would be upset for a little while longer, but at least then they could get over me and move on.

My mom did her best not to leave me home by myself, but one night I found myself alone in my kitchen looking out at the lake I lived on. Thoughts came and went in my clouded mind. The worst part was that I was unable to even think hard because my mind would reset when I tried. I was the saddest and lowest I had ever been, stripped of even my own mind. Unable to process complete thoughts, fragments of realities flooded the forefront of my mind like waves on a beach. I felt submerged under the riptides, tossed and turned by the waves, gasping for air.

I began to think more seriously about giving up. I decided that drowning was the easiest way to do it. People would be sad and disappointed, but they were already so sad and disappointed, and life was so painful. I had no vision for my life ahead of me. I was too tired to imagine I had to live like this forever. It was an eerie autumn night as I looked out of our kitchen window. The light of the sun had slipped behind the trees, leaving the lake black in color.

All I could do was sit there. I couldn't read with double vision. Watching TV would hurt my eyes even more. I couldn't call anyone because that would just burden them more. I was so disgusted with myself, and I was so hurt. I had to make a change. I had to get rid of myself.

I was drowning and had a choice to make.

I looked back out over the lake and began to see my life very clearly. Where I had only seen one, hopeless path for my life, I saw two paths stretch before me. It was a great change from my clouded mind just moments before, as God had stopped the waves for one sobering moment.

One path was death and the other was life. Death looked and felt exactly like I did. Nothing. It was dark. It was jagged, yet somehow comfortable. It was less that I wanted that path and more that I believed it was where I belonged because I no longer cared if I lived or died. I just wanted the pain and disappointment to end. I was done fighting. My body was exhausted. I was done making myself and everyone else deal with how disgusting I was.

As I saw the other path stretch out before me, the path of life looked exactly like death in the foreground. It was dark, jagged, and painful. But something about life was different. There was a small spark of light at the end of the path. I knew without a shadow of a doubt that the light was Jesus.

I knew choosing life would mean choosing an identity that was not bound by circumstance, even though I had no idea what that meant yet. It was terrifying. I knew I would have to step into the starkness of my empty future and see hope with different eyes. Choosing life meant I would have to come to terms with seeing God's blessings separate from God's promises. God does not promise I will succeed in my plans or be healed on earth, but He promises us purposes we may not have seen before. I had no idea what it would look like, but I knew through faith I could blindly trust God with my life.

I felt like Peter in Matthew 14:30, sinking in the waves: "Lord, save me!"

Jesus looked at me struggling in the waves: "Are you drowning?"

What a funny question to ask. Of course I was drowning. Couldn't He see that?!

But at the same time, it was beautifully filled with grace like a teacher during an exam who asks a question that brings forth a deep truth unlocking the answer: I knew how to survive.

I had to stop fighting the riptide. I should've stopped fighting it months ago, and my time was almost up.

The choice was mine for the making. It was the biggest choice of my life. I was holding onto the past, thinking *that's* what God wanted. I was vehemently against choosing the path of laying down every part of who I used to be up until that point, not knowing God was asking me to lay all of it down. But God didn't want me for what I could do; He just wanted me.

Choosing to live when every day was filled with pain and nausea would mean I would no longer live for my own purposes. Did I want to still live life if it would truly not be my own? Was God worth it?

I knew His plan was for me to live because I was still alive, but was God worth that level of trust?

Would I trust that God loved me, even when I couldn't find a reason for Him to? Would I trust that God is who He says He is, even when I don't feel Him at all? The Prince of Peace, my Healer, the Lord of all creation was with me, yet I was still so broken.

I knew God had never abandoned me, but He seemed so silent. It was as if my head knew of God, but my heart felt distant.

God saw that I was drowning in the waves. I was that little girl again at the beach, fighting the riptides as hard as I could. I was using all my energy to fight something so much stronger than I was.

I looked to Jesus and His outstretched hand, and I let myself go.

Though I chose life, this choice would continue to challenge every part of me. The mentality exuded by so many successful athletes and businesspeople at the apex of their careers said, "Never give up on your dreams" and "Hard work beats talent if talent doesn't work hard." But this was literally killing me. And since I was now unable to attain those dreams, I was the villain of my story, or at least my symptoms were. I had to redefine the villain and reset good vs. evil.

The Bible tells us there is real evil out there in the world, and I am not the one to blame for my suffering (John 9:1-4). I am not the true villain because I had the accident. If that was true, I should get rid of the villain and be done with it.

The accident isn't the true villain, either.

The villain was the creator of the lies I had believed, the father of lies (John 8:44). It's the one who whispered in my ear as I laid in bed, saying that I would be better off dead than alive. It's the one who wants to cause me further harm.

This made me realize a very important truth that contrasted the attitude I had lived by: it may take more strength to not give up on yourself than it would to not give up on your dreams.

Being unsinkable in the waves of life as I trusted Jesus would mean I would not drown even when the waves were pulling me under. It was the way my life would be saved, but also the way my life as I had known it would be lost forever. Although I would not drown, I would have to give up all control. I would have to let the riptides of life push me in a frightening and unwanted direction, but there was a promise that I would survive.

I realized that death would be fulfilling my desires to give up and that choosing life was what God was asking me to do. Death was the end of the road toward achievement, and life meant something different. In a strange way, choosing life felt like the most selfless thing I had ever done. It was a decision I was making for God, with God.

I did not want to keep living in pain, and every new day meant another day filled with things I did not want. However, it did not matter how low I got, because I knew God would be there with me, even if I could not feel Him. He would be there as He had been my entire life. I had to trust God because I knew deep in my soul He was worthy of that trust.

I stood up and made my way to my room, holding the walls to stay balanced. I grabbed my Bible and went back to that same kitchen table seat. I didn't really know why I got my Bible. I wouldn't be able to read it, but I knew the living word of God had the answers I needed. I didn't think I had any more tears to cry, but I surprised myself. The tears hit my Bible as I said a simple prayer, something like:

"God, you are light. I know that I know that I know that, but I don't see it. Be that light in me. I don't feel anything. I don't feel you at all. I feel so alone. I know you somehow must love me because you love everyone… I don't feel that love, and I don't see it… although I also know it to be true because I believe you are who you say you are. How could you possibly love me when I have so disappointed you? I know you are peace no matter the situation…I don't feel any peace. I know you are hope when all hope is lost, and right now, all hope is lost. I have no hope. Have your way in me. Have your way."

Looking back, I did die that night. The insecure, performance-driven, accomplished teenager who knew what she wanted out of life had left me. The grieving process for her had just begun, as she slipped away from my tight grasp like an object melting in my hand.

I died and no one came to my funeral,
I stood there all alone.
Crying and weeping, everything was gone,
Not just my life, but everything I had known.

I died and no one came to my funeral,
What's worse, they think I'm alive.
They see me in pictures, memories, and places,
They didn't know I hadn't survived.

My smug, dead face in the casket,
Made me scream, "WAKE UP! I NEED YOU STILL!"
The silence turned to a ring in my ears,
And my breath gave out after shrills.

How could I live when I had just died?
I sat in the graveyard alone.
I was a numb shell that needed to be filled,
Something I could not do on my own.

A carpenter appeared in the graveyard garden,
The one who handled my casket with care.
He told where I could fill my shell,
And the opportunity I had was rare.

I died and no one came to my funeral,
Except I saw the carpenter had been there.
Watching and waiting with love in His eyes,
It would be a long road, but I would repair.

Chapter 10

COMPARISON

I t is nothing short of iconic in the show *The Office* when Michael Scott walks out of his office and screams, "I DECLARE BANK-RUPT-CY!"

Only a few moments later, Oscar, the accountant, walks into the room and explains you can't just say that you are bankrupt and expect anything to happen. There is paperwork and an entire process to embark upon.

Michael looks at Oscar and says, "I didn't say it. I *declared* it."

Although this is just a humorous line from a show, it felt similar to how I was living my life. I had decided and declared that life was worth living, but this didn't make me automatically feel secure in my bare-bones identity in Christ.

One of the biggest obstacles to living a life of peace in God's purposes was an enemy called comparison. This was because, for me, feeling worthy was all about how I fit into what other people were capable of and if I gained others' approval. Am I smart? Well, it depends on who else is in my class. Am I athletic? Not if I've lost every game I played recently. Am I doing well in life? If those who I respect tell me I am, then I am.

I did not attend the all-day, everyday program in the city because other therapies I was currently in, like vestibular therapy, seemed more promising at the time.

Each time I walked into my vestibular therapy room, I was bombarded with the sight of my peers: eighty- to ninety-year-old men and women. They were my colleagues, so to speak, who were receiving the same treatment. Sitting next to an eighty-nine-year-old woman whirling through the same exercises I was having so much trouble with was just depressing. I spent sessions crying and asking myself what others would think if they knew how poorly I was doing. Defeated didn't even begin to describe how I felt. I was supposed to be in college. I was supposed to be playing a collegiate-level sport. I was not supposed to be on the verge of throwing up from simply moving my head in a specific direction to look at another letter on the wall, as my therapy required.

I felt the Holy Spirit guiding me to stop comparing myself to others. I couldn't change how other people saw me, but the Holy Spirit could change how I saw myself.

It came back to a simple idea: life isn't all about me. It wasn't a harsh recognition; it was freeing.

I started to see how self-focused I was at my deepest low points. When I was in those moments of utter despair and self-loathing, I was thinking only about myself. Being obsessed with hating myself was still being obsessed with myself.

Comparison seemed self-focused too, as I was restricting how I saw others: better than me or worse. Much like forgiveness, I had to take a step down from my judgement throne and give God the golden scepter. God is the judge, not me.

The fact that an eighty-nine-year-old woman was physically

outperforming me said nothing about my value or what God was doing in my life. The first step was recognizing that berating myself in circumstances like that was evidence of comparison. The second step was learning to stop those trains of thoughts after I recognized them. I didn't know when I would get better or if I would. Comparing myself to someone who had more than me would not be able to motivate me in this condition.

Every time I had the chance, I would ask and ask and ask for examples of people who had accidents like mine to be compared to, so I could find a path toward healing. But doctors kept saying things like, "Once you treat one person with a brain injury, you have treated one person with a brain injury." This means that every person's recovery is vastly different from another's. I was being called to live in just my own recovery.

I failed to improve after several months of vestibular therapy, so the doctors recommended we turn our attention to my vision issues. I was often asked after the accident what I thought my "main" problem was, and I almost always said my eyes. They ached and hurt in light one hundred percent of the time, varying from "painful" to "excruciating," and something was just off. Sometimes I would see with blurry vision, and other times I would see double. My best way of explaining it was simply saying that they were "just not quite right." My vision was fine before the accident, so I knew everything I was experiencing was due to the injury. We had been to optometrists and ophthalmologists and even a neuro-ophthalmologist, but all the tests came back inconclusive.

The neuro-ophthalmologist recommended we schedule a more thorough consultation with an eye institute in New York City that "does wonders," so I endured another horrible, nausea-filled ride into the city. As we got out of the car, my eyes stayed nearly shut because it was so painful to open them. My parents each grabbed one of my arms to steady me, and we walked into one of the best eye institutes in the world.

I took scores of diagnostic tests, all of which made me nauseous to the point of vomiting and dizzy to the point of falling down. My eyes were in such pain as we worked with the doctors to get the needed information.

After reaching my limit of diagnostics, we waited in the office for the doctor to come in.

She was very friendly, but seemed less enthusiastic after reviewing my charts. "I took a look at your testing," she said, "and I want to do a couple more things even though the nurse told me how the tests you've already done made you sick. It's going to take a lot to get you back to accounting."

Holding on for dear life, I took the last few tests and threw up. Afterward, the doctor came back to tell us my results.

Words and diagnoses we had never heard of flew around the room so fast we saw only shadows. Severe convergence insufficiency, oculomotor dysfunction, accommodative spasm, asthenopia, photosensitivity, severe accommodative insufficiency, visual vestibular dysfunction, visual perceptual deficits, diplopia, severe deficit in visual memory/processing speed, convergence palsy, and more.

Finally, we were at a doctor who could define and quantify my visual impairments. It was simultaneously daunting and refreshing.

Up until that point, most of my symptoms made no sense to me, except for some neurological connections made by my neuropsychologist. Now, though knowing visual symptoms had names was the furthest thing from comfortable, it somehow seemed a lot more secure. Problems with names seemed more likely to have actual solutions.

"It's going to take a lot of work to get Jenna better, but I really think this will help her," the doctor said with confidence. This seemed much more hopeful than things we had heard in the past.

"Whatever it takes," my dad replied with tears in his eyes, and my mother nodded in reassurance.

My ears had perked with interest as vision therapy was now on the table. I liked the sound of working to get better. I loved work.

Sure, other therapies did not work in the past, but cognitive therapy, vestibular therapy, and physical therapy turned me away because my vision hampered what I could do in those therapies. I had thrown up and put so much effort into those therapies for seemingly nothing, but now there was new hope in vision therapy. Once my vision was better, I could attack vestibular therapy and cognitive therapy a second time and see results.

I left the office feeling physically terrible but more encouraged than ever. I knew vision therapy meant there would be a lot of pain ahead. But if more pain now meant I would feel better later, I would do it in a heartbeat. There was a part of me that thought, *OK, this is going to be how God chooses to heal me.*

As we prepared to make our way back out of the city, we stopped at a local Starbucks about a block away so that my mom could grab a coffee. It had been a physically and emotionally exhausting day for both of us, and she grabbed me a pink cake pop, my all-time favorite, to drown out the taste of puke.

I took a picture of the pretty pop near Bryant Park, with the business buildings in the background reflecting cool blues and greens off one another. I was inspired by how beautiful the colors were. I felt God's presence in the hues and in the sweetness on such a sour day. Sitting on the cold, hard, dirty street to balance myself, I uploaded the photo to Instagram with the caption, "Cake pops city style."

Muscle memory had guided my fingers to post correctly. Once again, no one would know the truth behind the post. I wasn't posting inaccurate representations of my life on purpose; I just loved the colors amidst the squinting and pain. I knew that when I would look back on my feed, I would see God's promise of sweet peace during such a painful day. Would it be better to post a picture of me puking on the street? I loved finding the beauty in each day, especially the difficult ones.

My mom held me up as we made our way to the parking garage. With sunglasses blocking some of the light-sensitivity, I kept my gaze looking only toward the ground and did my best to avoid walking into anyone by watching people's feet come in and out of my sight. Clinging to my mom, I almost completely lost my balance with each passing block.

I glanced up as we stopped to wait for traffic to pass by. Standing in front of me was a man who looked homeless. It is common to see homeless men and women in midtown Manhattan, but something was different about this man. I knew my eyes were struggling to see correctly, so I could not help but stare for far longer than was socially acceptable.

In one surreal moment, I realized he had no eyes. Perhaps he was born that way because there was no scarring, just flesh where his eyes should have been. As my own eyes throbbed in pain, I stood in shock. I continued to look at this man as my mom, still holding my arm, moved forward into the stopped traffic. After the long day at the doctor, I had no processing ability left to make sense of what I had just seen, so I left that man on a shelf somewhere in my memory I knew may or may not be there when I would go looking for it.

But a few days later, I did find that memory and told a family friend about the man with no eyes. Their immediate response was an exclamation: "Wow! God put that man in front of you on purpose so you could see how blessed you are to still have eyes! You at least can see, and that man can't!"

I was puzzled and probably did not say too much as a response, as I let the idea of what they had said linger for quite some time.

I thought a lot about how comparing yourself to someone with less can lead you toward thankfulness. Thankfulness draws us closer to God and is essential to our relationship with Him. It can change our hearts and minds in a good direction perhaps more than anything else. However, this just didn't sit right with me. Should I be using this man's disability to attain thankfulness for myself?

Though comparing myself to someone who has less may invite thankfulness, it does not necessarily invite worship of God. I realized that I had always connected abilities to my identity. In my own heart, I lost my ability to be worthy of God's love when I lost my abilities. I had to reset and see worth in the midst of inability. God was sharing a truth with me that would become a backbone for my life: *You don't need what you don't have in order to fulfill God's plan for your life.* Knowing I didn't need what I didn't have is part of an unwavering, eternal foundation. It was sort of the antidote for wanting to be anyone else but myself. I didn't want my worth as a person to be swayed by my circumstances anymore, driven by comparison to people who I judged as being worse or better off than I was.

Even though this truth was food for my soul, I was still daunted by the prospect of moving on toward a different path.

Chapter 11

JENNA 2.0

"The Ghost of Who I Used to Be"

There's a ghost that haunts my days and dreams,
I want it to go, but know not how it leaves.

It came when a part of me was taken and died.
And only what was left of me had survived.

Its sickening embrace pretends to comfort me.
It calls me home, to how things used to be.

It reminds me of the "me" I once wanted to be,
But I am stuck with only what I can see.

But enough is enough, I want it to leave.
I have had enough time to wallow and grieve.

Today is the day I say goodbye to my ghost,
I am through with this sorrow and will not be its host.

Goodbye to the "me" I used to know,
And goodbye to the path I used to follow.

I look to my right and blaze a new trail,
One that is scary; I could easily fail.

With no ghost above me, I now see the sun,
I not only begin, but I start to run.

Exchanging gifts with Matt later that year during Christmas of 2014 became a memory we sometimes look back on and chuckle about, although there was no laughing that day. I had just told him how excited I was about starting one class at a school near my house with a great business program. Though I had conceded to the fact that I wasn't healthy enough to return to my old school for my sophomore year, my family and I had agreed that I could take one class locally, starting in the spring semester. Matt became excited for me too, and when we exchanged gifts at Christmas, one of my last gifts from him was oddly shaped. I smiled at his wrapping paper performance and opened it with curiosity and excitement.

I saw a t-shirt and mug with my new school's name in letters, loud and proud. The room was spinning and falling out from under me in its usual ways, and nausea was creeping up my throat as it always did. My mind was so clouded, but then all in one instant as I looked at the letters, I heard my mind say, "This is your life now." I must've blankly stared at the gifts for about a full minute before bursting into tears.

I wish I could tell you it was one glistening tear down my cheek. We sat in his dorm room, looking out over the gorgeous New York City skyline view, and I cried in heaves. My body was shaking, and poor Matt felt like he had ruined Christmas.

I had been outwardly positive about my new school because I was trying to make myself feel better about the transition. My first school was my dream school: a small Christian school with a great accounting program and tennis team where I felt comfortable and fit in. My new state school was more than twice the size with the completely opposite feel.

Perhaps more than that, something about taking a class at my new school made me think I had to truly be done with the idea of going back to my old life. Graduating on time would now be impossible, even if I did wake up one day and feel better. I had failed. Everyone was moving on without me, and my friends would be graduating earlier than me. While taking one class was a great step and accomplishment, it felt more like failure.

Matt and I prayed together about what I was feeling. While it was OK and even healthy to mourn over what had happened to me, the feelings of failure were not coming from a good place.

In order to reorient my worldview to God's there were two more people I had to stop comparing myself to: my old self and my future self.

Seeing my "now" self as my "forever" self, made my whole future look hopeless. I wanted to relate with the version of me that I was as a seventeen-year-old girl, not myself today. I wanted to be her, but I could feel her slipping further and further away. It didn't help that every doctor I went to literally asked me to compare my symptoms before and after the accident.

I felt like God was asking me a new question: "Do you trust me that 'Jenna 2.0', as you are right now at this moment, has just as much value and worth as 'Jenna 1.0?'"

To be honest, my answer was still a resounding no.

I dreaded the idea of newness. I did not want January to come when people would talk about a new year, new resolutions, and new life. My birthday was now an unwanted occurrence leaving me with dread and discomfort because another year would leave me further and further from who I used to be.

I felt myself shrinking away when I read verses like Isaiah 43:19:

> "See, I am doing a new thing!
>   Now it springs up; do you not perceive it?
> I am making a way in the wilderness
>   and streams in the wasteland."

I asked God to completely change my mindset. If I was going to remain alive for Christ on earth, this needed to change. I needed a strong foundation of truth. Through reading my Bible in very small increments and constant prayer, I kept reminding myself of the truth God had given me to stand on. I would repeat the words: You don't need what you don't have in order to fulfill God's plan for your life.

Then one day, I felt the words build up to more: You don't need what you *used to have* in order to fulfill God's plan for your life.

I welled up with tears. It seemed so simple and so similar to what helped with my comparison to others, but I knew God was giving me truth in bite-sized portions. God was not asking me to have what I used to have. God's goal was not necessarily for me to get back to who I used to be. Why? Because He does not need me to be a different version of my current self for me to be worthy to Him or for Him to fulfill His will through me. Surrendering my heart was all that He wanted from me.

Slowly, He started to show me more about His scale of worth. I began to realize that instead of looking backward or forward at the past or future me, He was trying to get me to look at where I was right then. This new realization was liberating. God was showing me that I was taking all the value out of who I was now by comparing myself to who I was before.

Comparing myself to an older, more perfect self or a future, more perfect self was such a problem because while I saw the good in the past and good in the future, I saw only the bad parts in the present. I realized that, accident or not, this was a trap I could live in my entire life. Always looking back or always striving forward was leaving me discontented with myself currently. God was calling me to live in the now, by the words of worth and truth He spoke over me about what I need to fulfill His plans for my life.

Chapter 12

STRENGTH IN WEAKNESS

This new semester of spring 2015 was nothing like before the accident. The school was working to provide the accommodations I needed to get through lectures, note-taking, study sessions, and exams for my single class. It was slow-moving and exhausting, but being back at school felt right.

I still struggled to the same extent with comprehension, and my vision was greatly impaired. I had a very limited store of energy to go out and do anything physical. Usually, if I wanted to be able to do any sort of low-key social activity after going to class, I had to get in a solid, half-day nap beforehand to recharge. Then I also had the exercises, therapies, and routines I did to work on my physical recovery. Class was one day, vision therapy was the next, and it rotated back and forth. My mom would drive me to class or therapy and then drive me home, at which point I would go right to bed. I learned to not make any plans during the day, because I usually ended up having to cancel anything other than school and therapy anyway. My body did not let me do anything more as I would collapse to sleep after therapy or class. The semester inched by, and though it was super difficult, God was carrying me through.

I woke up one afternoon from a much needed post-class nap, excited to attend the Christian group on campus. I had gone a couple of times before and had gotten to know a few of the people in the group. There were probably only about seven to ten committed members in the whole school who would call themselves Christian, so the group was like an oasis of people with similar faith. I tried to perk myself up, as I reapplied my red lipstick and took a deep breath.

After getting to school, I walked to the group and prayed silently. I asked God to use me and to move among our group. I turned around and saw a guy smoking close by and I decided I would invite him in. He looked at me with eyes like daggers and said, "What did you say was meeting tonight?"

A little caught off guard by his intensity, I smiled and said "Oh, it's our Christian fellowship group! You're welcome to come! We have free pizza!"

He looked at me puzzled, and said very sternly, "Well, I am Muslim."

I smiled and said, "Well, you're still welcome to come! And I hope you do!"

He looked into the distance and then back at me. "Fine. I will come right after I finish this cigarette."

I went in ahead of him feeling a little overwhelmed about the imminent conversation about Christianity I was going to probably have with someone who didn't share my beliefs at all. Before the accident, I would have been ready with all sorts of facts and points about Christianity that I had learned in high school, but this was not going to be possible in my current state.

I had never felt more unqualified in my life, yet I had such confident peace. I knew that if God still wanted to use me in spite of my difficulties, he would.

I took a deep breath. *I don't need what I don't have in order to fulfill God's plan for my life. I don't need what I used to have either.* We sat on the side and introduced ourselves. The next thing he said to me was, "I'm actually not Muslim. I am an atheist because if there is a God, I hate him."

I just nodded and said, "OK, tell me more."

He talked about his family and how close he was to them. He exclaimed that his mother prays five times a day to a god that has done nothing for her. He went on to talk about how bad things happen in the world, and he hates God for doing those things. He shared in depth about his life story and how it shaped his view of the god he didn't believe in anymore.

I remember taking a deep breath, looking up to God in prayer for answers and then seeing that my response to the deep spiritual, philosophical, and personal questions that he presented could come from my personal experience and what God had been teaching me since the accident.

I talked about how a terrible thing happened to me, but God was carrying me through. I explained how much I lost and described my current quality of life, finding myself utterly confused more often than not, throwing up, and being in bed so often. I explained that I did not want any part of this life if not for Jesus because He gives me purpose and hope in His presence.

We discussed so many deep issues, and I continued to pray and respond just by simply recounting my story and what God specifically spoke into my heart when I had similar questions like:

"How do you know God loves you?"

"Why does it feel like God isn't answering my prayers?"

"What's the point of life?"

"Why am I even here if I can't do the things I am certain I was put on earth to do?"

At the end of our conversation, he looked at me very seriously. He leaned in and told me he had something that makes him feel the way I feel with Jesus. He said this thing makes him happy and that it fills him with gladness, pleasure, joy, and love when he is consumed by it. It has the power to turn any situation around.

Truthfully, I was a little scared to hear what this could possibly be, and my mind raced trying to figure out what it was.

Eventually, he told me that this thing was music.

In my head, I prayed, "God, I know you're better than music, and you know you're better than music, but really quick please…how are you better than music?"

Then, just as easy as all the other answers had come for me, God showed me what to share with my new friend.

I looked at him and said, "Well, are you using music to escape?" He leaned in closer with the emptiest eyes I have ever seen and said, "Aren't we all trying to escape?"

I looked at him as the peace of Jesus was funneling out of me. "Honestly, no. I am not trying to escape," I replied. Even I was surprised by my words. After sharing with him how terribly I felt each and every day and all that I had to give up and will continually have to give up throughout life, I explained that I was not trying to escape my life.

Using something to escape your situation is only retreating to a place where you can forget about your problems, until they inevitably come back. Going to Jesus is looking at your biggest fear and problem head-on and feeling peace, even if it does not go your way.

Peace is a person. Love is a person. Hope is a person. I told my friend it's not something I could explain other than asking Jesus into your heart and figuring it out for yourself. It takes trust and faith, but God meets you where you are. It is not a mystical or magical experience; it is prayer, like talking to a loved one and confidant.

I never saw that person again, but I like to think that we both left the group better than we came.

The breezes of night hit my face as I waited for my mom to pick me up. I was amazed at how God had used me. I believe my friend's faith (or lack thereof) was deeply challenged. At the beginning of the conversation I had thought, *Why me?* as in *Why did God want me to be the one to talk to him?* If this man had questions about God, wouldn't He want to use someone who went to school as a theologian? Leaving the group that night, I thought, *Why not me?*

I saw that the "new thing" God was doing was using my weakness instead of my strength. My responses to the deep questions of life all came from my profound physical weakness and hope in God. I came across 2 Corinthians 12:9 at that time: "'My grace is sufficient for you, for my power is made perfect in weakness.' Therefore I will boast all the more gladly about my weaknesses, so that Christ's power may rest on me."

This verse finally made sense for the first time. My weakness was a way for me to connect with others, not a point of shame. Perhaps His power works best in weakness because when weak people overcome, it could only be through God.

It reminded me of the man without eyes from a few months ago. God very well may use that man in greater ways than someone with 20/20 vision. This meant that comparing myself to him to feel better about myself was not only belittling him, but also belittling what God could do in his life.

For the last year and a half, I had seen myself as a benched athlete on "God's team" (if I was even on that team at all), but God was now shattering that lie.

There's no bench on God's team. In fact, God's team isn't like a sports team at all, it is a body.

"The human body has many parts, but the many parts make up one whole body. So it is with the body of Christ... The eye can never say to the hand, 'I don't need you.' The head can't say to the feet, 'I don't need you.' In fact, some parts of the body that seem weakest and least important are actually the most necessary" (1 Corinthians 12:12, 21-22 NLT).

God sees purpose in the way He created each part of us. Our

bodies and appearances give us all unique ways to interact with others. Our abilities or lack of abilities make us strive toward community, which is what He intended.

God didn't judge me the way I judged myself and saw beauty where I saw ugliness, rotting, and decay. I saw that I had a purpose in His body, even if I used to be a hand and now I was more of an internal organ.

I embraced the mystery of God as I simultaneously clung as hard as I could to the truths I had learned.

Literally unable to get up out of bed, I would feel God inviting me to pray. Bits and pieces of prayers would come through my mind as the resets would leave me blank and force me to start over. It was OK, though. God wasn't asking me to be anyone else or do anything I couldn't. I didn't need what I didn't have, and I didn't need what I used to have.

A person's name would flash through my mind. I would begin to pray for them. Grabbing my phone, I would text the person I had prayed for. I would shut my eyes as my muscle memory would direct my fingers to the appropriate letters. Trying to read my text was hard, but God wasn't asking me to read the text. God was asking me to pray and reach out.

God gave me so much purpose in those moments. So many times, the person that came to my mind was at a critical moment or breakthrough point in their life, unbeknownst to me. How did I know? I didn't. I had just surrendered to God's leading.

Praying was sometimes the only thing I could do, but prayer changes things. Prayer to the God of all creation is powerful. Over the course of years, I saw lives transformed and was deeply moved by how God had answered my prayers. I was home, but I was able to support the other parts of the body of Christ in this way.

I used to think that when God looked at each person, there was one big purpose He saw for each individual. However, I grew to realize our lives are filled with infinite, multifaceted purposes. In addition,

I wonder if some of the smaller or less significant instances of purpose may not be so insignificant at all.

What an amazing picture of our God. In the midst of our inadequacies, in the midst of our pain, God shows up and shows us how He is there, how much He thinks of each of us right where we are, and how He has a plan to use us and our lives for the good of His kingdom. God would be able to make some good out of all of this, even if that didn't include my physical healing on earth. The way He was healing my heart to make me open to His will and His plans showed me how much He had in store for me even when I thought I had nothing left to give.

Chapter 13

GOD EQUIPS THE UNEQUIPPED

There are some weekends that even with my memory lapses, I will never, ever forget. My family was in Vermont, staying at a friend's house. Everyone else was skiing, but my mother and I went into town to shop for a short time until I would need to take a break and nap. I had always loved to ski, so my heart ached for the slopes. I had been on skis since I was able to walk. Even though skiing was practically second nature to me, it was totally out of the question after the accident. There was no safe way for me to get on a ski lift or exert my body with that much exercise, even on the bunny hill. But I knew I could not spend every day crying about things I could not change. God was giving me strength for each moment. Little did I know, just over a year and a half after my accident, things were about to take another devastating turn for my family.

We were in the Lilly Pulitzer store in Manchester, Vermont, the day we got the call. Jacob, my brother, had just gone to the doctor a few days before and the impending "what ifs" were lingering in the air.

My mom's cricket-noise ringtone went off, and I stopped looking at dresses and went close to her side: it was the doctor. She answered the phone and the words sounded fake. We sat on the ground and welled up with tears—Jacob had cancer. It took our breath away. All of a sudden, nothing that used to matter to us before seemed like a problem now. Thankfully, the store was not crowded, because we sat in the corner of the upstairs sale annex for quite some time.

The days came and went as he underwent surgery and more bloodwork. Now, Jacob and I were both home on our couch recovering. We were both in pain. We were both in need of my mother's constant attention as we recovered. For a few weeks, neither of us were able to drive, so she drove us both to our college classes. Mine were held on the other side of the county, and Jacob's were about forty-five minutes away. It was surreal, but in a way it felt natural that we were all together. Jacob was the visionary, and I was the accountant. That's always how our relationship was. My junior year of high school, he was the President of the National Honors Society, and I was the Vice President. He had the vision for the group, and I followed up with the details. He had enough confidence for the both of us.

Jacob and I were one year apart in school because he has a June birthday, but almost two years apart in reality. We are "twenty-one months apart," as my mother would say. We had always been close growing up so having Jacob at home was like having a friend by my side. Our days were filled with trying to do schoolwork in more pain than we expected, lots of prayer, many episodes of Seinfeld, and a lot of laughter. Some days were so sad that we could not help but laugh. It did not feel like this could even possibly be our reality.

It was around this time that I learned that painting reduced my symptoms and made my body calm down more than almost anything else, including sleep. Why I even tried to paint will always be a mystery to me. I think I always liked art, but I was never any good at it. Somehow, this all changed after the accident. I realized that anything I tried to draw, I could draw. It was such a sudden onset of skill that it surprised and confused me. If I tried to draw a piece of fruit or an animal it would look like just that, instead of blobs and scribbles on the page. Soon, painting became my go-to activity between bouts of throwing up from a homework assignment. Math was so physically painful to focus on for even a few minutes, but I could paint for half an hour or even longer. I felt like I was four years old as my dad hung my paintings up all around the house. We were all surprised at my new talent.

One afternoon, I looked up from my painting and said to Jacob, "Wouldn't it be cool if we could put something I drew onto a dress or something?"

"Why can't we do that?" Jacob replied, and J. Shotmeyer was born.

Starting a clothing company seemed like the perfect thing to do. Jacob and I had always wanted to start a company together, and it just made sense to do it now that we had so much time together.

We began to think about why we would start a company. What would it be about? What was making us want to do this?

We realized that it always came back to connection. We wanted to connect with others. If we were both home from school, there had to be other college kids home from school struggling too. With my renewed identity in Christ, I wanted to share with others that although I was far from OK physically, I was standing on sturdy ground spiritually. Jacob and I knew that although our circumstances were dramatic, we could relate with almost anyone's story because at some point each person goes through pain, unexpected circumstances, and a refining of identity.

I sat for hours at the small chess table in our family room as Jacob laid on the couch and my mom was doing chores or making dinner close-by. We spitballed plans, ideas, and visions. Next to me, I had my brand new watercolor paints and a supply of square paper to try my best to create a repeatable pattern.

I had no idea where to even start.

I would paint flowers, fruits, and other objects we liked, and then Jacob would upload them to photoshop and make the painting into a pattern.

He researched manufacturers constantly and was more than up for the challenge of making our dreams a reality.

I was open about how little I thought I could contribute. In 2015, I had never heard of one person like Jacob or me who started a clothing line or company. I had only stories of mega-famous brands like Kate Spade and Tory Burch to glean from. It was before influencers began to sell their "merch" or bloggers would create designs. Without anyone to look up to, I grabbed Jacob's hand and jumped off the cliff into the deep end.

I was wildly unequipped for this calling, but I knew in my heart that God was more than behind it.

We launched our first line of ties and bow ties, which eventually evolved into t-shirts and dresses. In between homework assignments and doctors' appointments, this became our happy place to be able to create and collaborate with purpose. We collaborated on everything.

In a time when so many doors were being shut, I just kept saying yes to the doors that were opening.

A year later in 2016, I found myself at a coffee shop in Hoboken, New Jersey, as a clothing designer.

My mom and I packed up our car with all the lemon-themed decorations we had been planning for months, and we made our way to the shop. Why? Because God had given us this dream to stand up and declare His name, even during our sour times.

The dresses arrived at my doorstep days before, and my mom and I ran to find our sizes to try on. I couldn't believe that something I drew was on a dress. I still couldn't believe that I could draw anything! We had dresses, t-shirts, ties, and bowties all set for the launch.

We had invited our family, friends, and lots of students from Jacob and Matt's school. We were so excited. Jacob figured out how to make our own Snapchat geofilter, and invitations were distributed all over Hoboken.

It was the most social I had been in months, if not years, which of course came with its physical setbacks. Still, the belief that God had a plan for this clothing line helped me push forward toward the launch with excited anticipation.

By the time it was my turn to talk that night, I was a shell of myself. I had been talking to people for a few hours, so my mind and stomach had almost completely escaped me. It was hard to stand straight, and even harder to not lose my train of thought. Thankfully, I did not need to know exactly what I was going to say or have anything memorized. Everything I was going to share was already my whole life and focus; I would do well to just share from the heart.

I took a deep breath and stood up on a bench in my lemonade dress and Kate Spade heels. I fixed my hair with my fingers, pursed my lips together with their fresh coat of red lipstick, and began.

"Welcome to our J. Shotmeyer launch party here in Hoboken…" I took a deep breath and quietly cleared my throat as I scanned the room. "Make Lemonade. Because, do you really have a choice? You're not someone who will complain until people can't hear it anymore. You're not someone who will let circumstances stand in the way of your happiness. You're not someone who will be defined by the mistreatment or hurt you have been given. You're an overcomer. You're a victor, a winner. You will rise up above this circumstance and make lemonade out of the lemons you are given. Why? Because you are amazing, and God has created you fearfully and wonderfully. Lemons look great on you!" Halfway through, I looked around the room and was deeply encouraged by the smiles looking back at me. I was so grateful for the chance to speak about something that meant so much to me. I continued on, confident in whatever words God brought to my mind.

"Thank you all so much for coming to our launch party. Tonight is about making lemonade out of the very difficult lemons in life that we receive. Within the print of the dress I painted and designed, there are little turtles to show it's natural for it to be a slow process to get to the point where we can make lemonade out of difficult circumstances. There are also lemon blossom flowers within the print to show how beautiful life can be when you decide to embrace the newness of the present moment. It's been a really hard process for me…"

I went into how difficult the last few years had been for me, how after the accident I felt like I was nothing, and how I only had one label to stand on, which was stronger than all my other labels combined. I stood as a walking testament that if I only had God's presence, it was enough for peace in my soul. I let the crowd in on how terrible I felt physically, but how God had created purpose through my very limited ability. I could not call manufacturers or discuss details of production, but Jacob could. He could not draw the patterns I was drawing, and neither of us could make our pain look beautiful like God could.

It would have been too much to explain how I had never wanted to be a designer and that I still wanted to be an accountant. It would have been too painful for me to share that I could no longer do math like I could before because the lines and numbers on the page were too hard for my eyes to see. I did, however, discuss what it was like to be a new artist and how God was using me within that space to minister to my heart and now perhaps theirs.

As I talked longer, I felt my nervous system shake more. It was very normal for me to feel like I was shaking on the inside, but when I saw my hands and legs visibly shake on the outside, I knew it had gotten worse. If they didn't see my memory lapses that I smiled through before, perhaps they would now. Really, it didn't matter. God was restoring my soul, and that was a testimony that I wanted everyone to have.

I looked out to the room full of guests and saw my brother's fraternity brothers listening to me intently. I saw girls who were struggling in their own ways to find their identity. I saw the guys from Matt's tennis team taking it all in.

God was continuing to use my brokenness to reach others, and somehow, that was beautiful. That was all I wanted, and He was granting my requests. I was not even close to being qualified or feeling like I was equipped enough for something like this, but just like God used people in the Bible, equipping them at just the right time, He was equipping and using me.

The whirlwind of the night came and went as we stood in the empty coffee shop after almost everyone had left. My mom brought her car around from a side street and a few friends helped us pack up. I grabbed someone's arm so I wouldn't fall down walking to the car. I would not be able to properly process what happened nor its impact for days as I recovered.

As I began to be able to look back through pictures and receive texts from friends, I realized that my ability to connect with others for Jesus was so much stronger than ever because of the story God had entrusted me with. When I explained what happened to me and what life was like every day, people were taken aback. I realized that my story was like a delivery of hope I could give to people, especially to people who were trying to stand on foundations that for me had been completely washed away.

My brother and I originally started J. Shotmeyer to reach out to others, but it grew into something that continued to sweeten our sour days. God used me beyond my ability as we hosted many pop-up shops, expanded our online store, and sold designs to boutiques. It was the most radical, strange, amazing, and wonderful surprise.

As our lives and company continued, Jacob got better and went back to his life cancer-free and forever changed. I, however, was forced to stay right where I was, but I continued to say yes to God.

It sort of felt like Jacob was spat out of the riptide, but I was still fighting for my life, being moved by the waves. I had the utmost respect for the horrible battle he fought, and no doubt was still fighting, even though he got to go back to his school and his "old life." As more days passed, an unsettling silence began to fill the empty space he had left in our house. I missed him more than ever. I missed his confidence in me. I missed him getting mad at me when I thought less of myself than I ought.

I guess his confidence in me—in us—was a crutch I could no longer lean on when he went back to living at school. I took solace in the hope that as God was equipping me for things like our company, He would continue to equip me for His callings regardless of who was physically by my side.

When I looked at the waves, I had nothing to be confident in. Most days, it sure looked like I could drown at any moment. But when I looked at the face of Jesus, I had more confidence than ever in my identity as a child of His. I am in charge of saying yes to the call, and God is in charge of how it happens.

One day on campus, I was approached by the Christian Fellowship group leaders, who happened to also be two of my closest friends at school. They wanted me to lead the large-group meetings for the next semester.

Almost startled, I quickly replied, "Um… no… I can't. I mean I physically cannot."

I was so weak that even just the fourteen-stair-step walk up to my room would sometimes leave me so out of breath and dizzy I would need to sit down on the floor right away. How could I lead a group?

They continued to encourage me as I reasoned aloud with them. I tried to go to the group regularly, but it was hard to even have the strength to go each week. Perhaps I could have just enough strength to attend every week if I planned my classes accordingly, but lead it?

"I literally cannot do it, guys…" I said to them, overwhelmed by the request. "I can't write the emails each week. I can barely read even one email…"

"I'll do the emails!" one of my friends said.

"OK, I can't go to the school club presidents' meetings. I won't have the energy…" I responded.

"I'll go to those!" said my other friend.

They explained that they were happy to do each and every other club-related task. They just needed someone to lead the discussion each week.

"Really?" I said, thinking this could possibly work.

The only thing that neither of them wanted to do was speak in front of people. I was so puzzled because there was only ever at most fifteen to twenty of us, but it was usually seven to ten of us. Sometimes, it was only two to four of us. I told them I would pray about it and get back to them.

Sometimes we ask God what we should do, and it feels like there is little to no response. Other times, we are told the response in every song that comes on the radio, every verse we read in the Bible, and every conversation we have with other people. This is what it felt like as my phone shuffled through my music and my Bible app chose the verse of the day. God was reassuring me in so many ways that this was my next step.

Leading a large group… really? But just like being a brand-new clothing designer, business owner, and artist, I put the pressure on God instead of myself. My identity didn't sink under those labels, because they weren't pointing to my ability. I am a Child of God, so the pressure to accomplish this would be on Him and work in His way.

I began to pray about what it would look like to lead a group. Right off the bat, God spoke to me about the number of students coming to the group. Each semester it seemed to dwindle, and we wondered each semester if it could be our last. It was pertinent that I do my best to get people to come, but also that I be content whether there was only one other person that showed up or if there were fifty. God didn't care about my definition of effectiveness as much as He did about my obedience and steadfastness to share His name on campus. Who was I to judge success in one of God's endeavors?

I counted the costs. I physically could barely read or concentrate. How in the *world* would I be able to speak to people who had never heard the Gospel? There were definitely more people on campus who were resistant to the Gospel than were open to it. It felt different than when I had talked to the atheist man about escapisms because this was not going to be a one-time event where God would show up. God was going to have to show up in our midst every single week.

I felt like God was calling me to it, but that didn't mean that my memory would not "reset." I would probably have all the problems I was having in this new context as well. What if I need to read a verse and I can't? What if I stutter and slur my speech if I get flustered or tired? I would be bringing very private embarrassments to a public setting each week. As it was now, I could show up to the group, say a few things when I felt like I could articulate, and most people would never know what was happening on the inside. Leading the group would indeed invite people in. Just because we say yes to God doesn't mean the path will be easy.

My circumstances gave a resounding *NO!* But my unsinkable identity pointed to my creator and helped me to say yes.

In the moment, I felt a stretching of faith and simultaneously a pull to what was comfortable and safe. My heart was in the epicenter of a battle.

The Bible talks about spiritual warfare in Ephesians 6:12: "For our struggle is not against flesh and blood, but against the rulers, against the authorities, against the powers of this dark world and against the spiritual forces of evil in the heavenly realms."

I felt this on campus. I felt it through anxiety and the lack of peace from my community of unbelievers. It was hard to be a Christian. Not because I was being persecuted or attacked by people, but because it was hard to feel the presence of God anywhere on campus. If I did not step up and trust God to equip me as the large group leader, I would continue to lack a community of believers around me. I needed to continue to form that community and pave a path for it to thrive.

I saw Psalm 37:4 as a promise: "Take delight in the Lord, and He will give you the desires of your heart."

If I was truly taking delight in the Lord and not myself, my full desire would be in alignment with God's desires. The Christian community that I had at my school and now longed for, may not be what I wanted it to be or look like, but I felt like Psalm 37:4 was a promise that God would equip me to lead the group meetings.

Before the semester started, it was my job to come up with a theme that would be carried through the entire semester for our group. It needed to be official, and it would be entirely based on what I came up with.

This part was exciting. What did God want to say to His children at my school? I prayed and prayed and prayed that God would speak to me and through me in this space.

Severely unequipped, I knew in my spirit that God was promising me that He would equip me for the plans He had for this group. I was reminded that I didn't need what I didn't have in order to fulfill this plan that God had set before me. I didn't need what I used to have, either.

The theme for the semester came easy to me: "God Equips the Unequipped."

It was perfect, because every time my mind would reset as I would feel mortified trying to lead ten other college students, I would be reminded through the scriptures that God would equip me.

Plus, I couldn't wait to learn about the handful of people in the Bible who were unequipped for the plans that God set before them. As I put together lesson plans, I realized that seemingly everyone in the Bible was unequipped for the plans of God. Perhaps that is the point. We are all unequipped. We are all a mere shadow of ability when compared to God. However, God within us proves to be radically strong.

The first lesson was on Moses, when God asked him, "Who makes a person's mouth?" I felt like I could identify with Moses as I led the study. It felt violating to lose my train of thought or start to stutter. In times like those, I looked down with double vision and made out the words, "God Equips the Unequipped," and I knew He was, therefore, equipping me. God made my mouth. He knew my ability and still asked me to lead the group.

We went through the stories of Abraham, Joseph, Ruth, Mary, David, and so many other men and women of the Bible. Over and over and over, God gave them exactly what they needed for what He was asking them to do.

The semester group meetings were a huge success in our hearts and minds as the Christian fellowship on campus. God moved in that room. He reaffirmed my foundation in Him as He equipped me each week to lead the conversation. The resets, stuttering, intense exhaustion, dizziness, and double vision did happen. But as I stepped out for God in obedience, He worked through me and in me.

Something that did not prove to be successful from the outside was the number of people who came. The numbers were low, but I didn't see this as a failure. In a school of about 6,000 people, eight was our solid weekly number. My two friends who encouraged me to lead the group went to the club fairs and kept up with the other tasks as promised.

I grew up believing that God would be more proud of me if I was the one who got the whole campus saved than if I ran a group that had only eight participants. However, I think that God is more so calling us to obedience. He is proud of my obedience whether He is asking me to pray for someone while no one else is around or if He is asking me to speak to 3 million people at once.

I continued to lead the large group, with each semester's theme different from the last. Each time, God equipped my desperately unequipped body for His will and purposes on campus.

This theme of God equipping the unequipped became so constant in my life it was almost laughable. I brought it up a few times a week in conversation for years and thought about it almost every day.

It was the way by which the fun and joyful things I did, like J. Shotmeyer and my leadership role within Christian Fellowship group, came to be. It felt like an old-fashioned life preserver that God threw to me in the waves. I clung to it with my whole heart. Sharing this message with others was like throwing them the very thing that was saving my life. This theme was also the way by which I endured the countless obstacles still in my path.

Chapter 19

MOMENT BY MOMENT

I was overwhelmed as I looked around the room. There were about fifty women milling about my friend's baby shower, and it seemed like they were all talking at the same time. I tried to listen to conversation within conversation to my right and left. The room began to move as I tried to concentrate. God had shown me that there could be purpose in my weakness, but it sure didn't feel like it when I couldn't even stand without nausea, dizziness, and a searing headache at a baby shower. I had to get out of it all.

"Jenna, WOW! Looking beautiful as ever! I love following all of your beautiful photos on Instagram! It looks like you're doing amazing!" one of my mother's friends said.

"Oh, thanks so much!" I responded with a pleasant smile while my eyes ached from trying to focus on the moving people around me.

According to Instagram, over this last year I had taken two semesters' worth of classes, gone to a few college formals with my boyfriend, and enjoyed a lot of life. They had no idea that even two and a half years after the accident, I could last only for about ten to twenty minutes in any given social, academic, or concentrated work situation before the puking would start. They didn't know that those two semesters included only three classes in total and that more of my time was spent in the vision therapy office than on campus.

I went to the bathroom and tried to calm my system down. I was shaking uncontrollably and felt like I was about to puke again. I begged the hopeless void to say it wasn't so. My thoughts were controlled and quiet, but no amount of breathing or telling myself to calm down could shake the nausea.

Most people told me they would just stay in bed if they felt that awful, but since this was my daily reality, I felt like I had to get out to stay sane.

I steadied myself and looked in the mirror and saw a sad, tired girl looking back at me. I was not supposed to hate myself anymore. "I gave that up, remember?" I whispered as my self-criticisms came to a halt. I slowly drew in a deep breath and let it out with a loud blow. Today is a new day, I reassured myself.

"Jesus, take this feeling from me, please. Show me the way," I prayed in a whisper.

It is only socially acceptable to retreat to the bathroom for a certain amount of time, so I pretended the break helped me feel better and went back into the sea of voices. I spied a place to sit across the room and moved to get there as soon as possible to steer clear of unwanted conversation.

An aunt I hadn't seen in a few years came up to me at the shower and exclaimed, "WOW! You've lost SO MUCH WEIGHT!!!" Someone else commented on how much shorter my hair was. I had been throwing up so much at therapy I had probably lost ten to fifteen pounds, even though I tried to eat as much as I could despite the nausea. My hair had fallen out and broken off due to the trauma, appearing much shorter than when I had gone off to school in 2013.

I never knew how to respond when people complimented me on my weight or commented on how different my hair looked, so I just smiled and nodded.

I was so used to being a social butterfly, flitting around a room and engaging people in all sorts of conversation, but that ability was long gone. Instead, I did my best to make as little eye-contact as possible and beeline somewhere I could sit so I didn't fall down.

The room moved like a boat as my eyes glazed over with fog. I was concentrating hard enough to prevent my vision from going double, but I would not be able to hold out for long. My visual clarity was gone, much like my mental state as I tried to process the words of those around me. The last thing I wanted to do was make a scene. I did not want to make the afternoon about me, so I tried to be invisible.

I found a seat on the ground, which was even better than my original plan since most of the ladies would not want to sit on the floor next to me.

I watched the beautiful mom-to-be open gift after gift and absorbed the happiness of my loved ones. Although I was happy to be at the joyous event, the searing pain made me wish the shower would end as soon as possible. From my spot on the ground, I began to imagine that I would be pregnant someday and hoped I would look as beautiful and calm as she did.

All at once my eyes became a dam holding back leagues of water. As my thoughts met my vestibular system, everything spiraled out of control as I let my guard down for just a moment. I compared the mom-to-be to my future pregnant self.

New levels of fear invaded my mind. Pregnant women get nauseous. If I were pregnant, how much more nauseous could I be? How would I keep *any* food down? Could I even attend my *own* wedding or baby shower? I did not see how I could possibly have a baby.

Perhaps I had not processed this before I was at a baby shower because I was not a girl who dreamed about being a mom. I was itching for the college and early-career stage. Of course, I would have told you I wanted to eventually get married and have a few children. My mother is the most amazing person in my life, so of course I wanted to be a mother. But my mother helped me with everything most days since the accident, driving me everywhere, reading me the menu at restaurants, and filling in the gaps where my memory failed me. What would I be able to help my child with? My symptoms made me bed-ridden for anything more than one event or task per day, so there was no chance I could be a mom. Children might not (or more pre-cisely, *should* not) ever be in the cards for me.

After most of the shower was finished, I stood up and left through a side door, grabbing the walls to help stabilize me. I texted Matt to come pick me up, because we had plans to hang out after the shower.

I could not even drive. How would I bring my kids anywhere?

I got in the car and squeezed Matt's hand. He says he cannot read my mind, but most days I don't believe him. From the driver's seat, he looked at me and smiled, "Love you, babe. It's going to be OK. I think you're doing everything right."

I welled up with tears and took a deep breath. Somehow, some-way, it was going to be alright.

It was in moments like this I had a choice to sit in my pain and fear, or pray and bring my concern before God. It was my choice to decide if I would invite comparisons of what my future self may (or may not) be capable of, or if I would rest in the promises of provision that come in moment by moment intervals. My spiritual growth in the last years had been palpable, even if my physical improvement hadn't changed. As I considered what my future may hold if my recovery trajectory didn't change drastically, it was so hard to not leave those all-important truths that were keeping me afloat in the deep currents.

I knew that God commands us not to worry about the future. He doesn't suggest it or advise it; He commands it many times in Scripture:

"So do not fear, for I am with you; do not be dismayed, for I am your God. I will strengthen you and help you; I will uphold you with my righteous right hand" (Isaiah 41:10).

"Therefore do not worry about tomorrow, for tomorrow will worry about itself. Each day has enough trouble of its own" (Matthew 6:34).

"Have I not commanded you? Be strong and courageous. Do not be afraid; do not be discouraged, for the Lord your God will be with you wherever you go" (Joshua 1:9).

As with any command, our choice is to obey or not to obey.

I had a choice: would I let this comparison between my friend and my future self cripple me or would I walk in the purposes of now? Would I be able to eat the provisions God was giving me today and trust that provisions for my future will come then? If it was God's will for me to have children later on, God would equip me then. I knew that. I did not need the provisions for the future in that moment because God would also be in the future. God was providing for me right now, so I had to trust the promise that He would provide for my tomorrows too.

At this time in my life, God did not entertain my pleas to know what my future would look like. Having no plans felt awkward and wrong. He did not release me to imagine if Matt would be my husband or just a college boyfriend. He did not let me know if I would ever live on my own, have children, or feel any better than right now. God's will for me was God and God alone. I could not put my trust in Matt, and I could not even put my trust in my mom although she helped me with everything. I wanted to reach for tangible things from God to feel more secure, but He just kept coming back to this pure white page with nothing on it, asking me to have faith. He was giving me all of the information I needed for the present moment alone, and as I fully trusted Him, my fear dissipated. It was the antidote for the anxiety that shook my chest and was my reference point as life spiraled out of control, even as I was taken farther and farther out to sea by the riptides.

Living moment by moment with Christ to alleviate my fears is not something I learned once and automatically put into practice. It's a daily decision I either actively choose or passively let slip by. The day of the shower, I made the decision to not mourn my future or to step into a place of fear. I praised God for His provision and thanked Him for His presence in my life. My worship turned my soul from fear to deep, unexplainable peace.

Chapter 15

WHAT'S ON YOUR RESUME?

I t isn't supposed to snow in April… but the cold wind against my cheeks told us otherwise.

The cold breeze pushed its way through the trees, sending a white veil that covered our vision as we got into the car for yet another appointment. The car was mainly silent for the couple hour drive as my parents, little sister, and I all made our way to a new doctor, a vocational specialist. This doctor was going to tell me what I would be able to do for a full-time job when I finally finished college.

I had given up most of my college dreams, but one dream I hadn't given up was my accounting major. As of yet, I hadn't needed to, so I moved with relentless determination toward the goal of graduating with this major, albeit slowly. However, I was beginning to question if I could actually get or keep any kind of accounting job. I still could barely look at a computer screen for more than twenty minutes without the room spinning uncontrollably and an episode of severe eye pain. How would I be able to create complex accounting spreadsheets in Excel?

Through the office of special services at my college, I was able to do my homework on gridded paper instead of on the computer. Some of my older professors didn't mind at all because this was how they used to do accounting before personal computers were invented. Because I was taking only one or two classes at a time, I was able to split up the homework into fifteen-minute sections and eventually get it done.

For exams, the office of special services would record the questions on an MP3 player and make large-print copies of the test so I could still manage to see parts of the sentences, even when my vision would blur or I would start to see double. They would break up my test into twenty-minute parts, allowing for me to run to the bathroom on a break or put my head down for as long as I needed. Sometimes I would even collapse out of dizziness on my way to the bathroom to puke. My memory problems were reduced the most in the mid-morning, so I would always plan to take the exam then. There were no snacks allowed, but I was able to bring ginger ale and protein which would help my mind if I had thrown up my breakfast during the test.

Usually, I would walk out of the testing room sure I had failed. Then, almost every time, I scored higher than the class average. It was baffling, but my success on paper was why I kept struggling through my major. If I had been feeling that terrible *and* failing my classes, perhaps I would've stopped trying to take them. But my grades were always enough to make me continue even though it was so hard on my body.

So many doors in my life were slammed shut, but my accounting major was a door with a crack leaking yellow light into the dark room. It was the smallest of cracks, but any light is enough to find your way when the rest of the room is pitch-dark.

I suppressed the fear in the back of my mind that the vocational specialist would tell me I needed to change my major. She would do her testing, and we would be able to find a good path. Even if specifically being an accountant was off the table for the time being, there had to be hundreds of jobs I didn't know about that I could do and maybe even other ways to use an accounting major.

As humbled and apprehensive as I was, I felt a deep, unexplainable peace from God in my heart. I trusted Him with my future. I knew that my vocation didn't dictate my worth, as I had always thought before. I knew my future was secure in Him.

We pulled up to her home office and just my mom and I went inside, leaving my dad and sister in the car. It was a dark, dank basement room turned into an office with a shag carpet that looked decades old. Eerie owl figurines covered the walls, all looking at me with their wise eyes of condescension. I'm not sure what I was expecting from the office of one of the best professionals in her field, but this was not it.

She asked me to perform several tests, and we went through an extensive list of question after question and exercise after exercise. My mind faded and the room began to spin and swirl as an all-too-familiar queasiness rose up in my stomach. I explained to the doctor that this was my post-accident normal.

She took some last notes and then began sharing her evaluation. I endured her retelling of the cruel details of my life that I already knew and waited with bated breath for her to say what kind of job I would be able to get. Fear of losing my accounting career crept up my throat like vomit. But God equips the unequipped, right?

The old woman with over thirty years of experience turned to me and looked me directly in the eyes. Nothing could have prepared me to hear the words that came out of her mouth.

"Well, I don't see how you would be able to hold down any sort of full-time job, let alone accounting." She outlined and detailed that class is a lot different than work. Work would require a full day of mental and physical stamina which I simply did not have. She went on to describe how even the easiest of jobs I would eventually be qualified for would not be something she could foresee me being able to do at a full-time level.

She mentioned that some government jobs are required to hire those with disabilities. Perhaps I could eventually do one of those jobs, if it were to be incredibly abbreviated, of course. She said that companies get grants for hiring people with disabilities, so sometimes they are happy to hire people knowing they cannot do a real job at the company. Perhaps there was a place that could take me on because they had to.

This was not just about accounting; it was about anything and everything. I was not qualified to fulfill any sort of full-time job. What?

I tried to refocus. This was me we were talking about. This was not theoretical. This was not just my next few years; this was my indefinite future. My dormant fears of being a burden to my family or future husband were now taking on new life. Turns out, I could be a burden to a company too. If I was lucky, I could be hired for a job I probably would not be able to even do just so the company could meet a quota. I had never thought of it that way.

I was numb. My mom and I walked toward the car with the little energy we had left, dodging the large snowflakes. It seemed as if the cold darkness was having its way, not leaving any room for spring to come.

I had so many thoughts that spiraled like the snow that hit my face. How was this happening? This wasn't the plan. This was not where I was supposed to be in life. This was not what I wanted. I never dreamed this could happen. It's not supposed to be this way. It's not supposed to snow in April.

In the car, we decided to go to Cracker Barrel for dinner. The ride over was mostly silent. My dad and sister must have known it was bad.

As we walked to our table, I could already feel the mac and cheese soothing the stomach acid burns in my throat. We sat down and ordered, but my mind wandered far beyond the menu at my table.

A lump the size of a large potato appeared in my throat and would not go away. Slowly at first and then all at once, the room spun faster, and I found myself crying uncontrollably. One or both of my parents grabbed me and brought me outside to the car as my body kept shaking and crying—crying from pain, crying from exhaustion, and crying from shock. I glanced at my little sister and felt bad yet again for dragging her through a boring doctor day that had turned into a meltdown. No middle schooler wants to spend her Saturday like that. I don't remember what my parents said to me because there wasn't much to say. The tears in both of their eyes made things worse, as I knew that I was disappointing them again. Here I was, practically an adult, uncontrollably losing it in a Cracker Barrel parking lot. Something was different about the sadness this time, though.

Although I was crying because the human perspective of the news made me so sad, I somehow still had a deep, dull peace that was the presence of God. Even though my outlook surrounding my physical life was much bleaker now than it had ever been, I did not go back to the empty hopelessness of years before. I was rattled, but somehow still firm.

I held onto Psalm 16:8 (NKJV), knowing that I will never be shaken: "I have set the Lord always before me, because He is at my right hand, I shall not be moved."

How? Because when I reeled myself back to the present instead of the future, I realized God was feeding me what I needed right then in that moment. It nourished me to realize I had the choice to trust He will do the same in my future.

I fell back on the secure foundation of my identity. It turned out to be the antidote for the fears that kept trying to attack me. I am a Child of God and don't need what I don't have in order to fulfill His plans for my life, and I don't need what I used to have. I have purpose and infinite worth with the exact amount of strengths and weaknesses I currently have. I could face this head on with peace because I fully trust God with my life.

My biggest fear was wrecked with something so much worse than I could have imagined, but I was still OK.

As much as I felt like I was living on a spiritual high at times, I

stayed grounded in the reality of my life. In addition to doctor appointments and treatments, I still had to answer friends' and advisors' questions about my future. This seriously challenged the commitment to
living moment by moment in the present.

How do you go to a vocational doctor and receive a terrible report
and then answer questions like, "What are you up to these days?";
"When are you going to graduate?"; "What do you want to do when
you graduate?"; "What is your five-year career plan?"; and "Where
do you see yourself in ten years?"

In pure irony, my presentation-based class that semester required
me to put together a talk that described myself and what I planned
to do after college. What was I supposed to say?

Presentation night came, and each student before me picked
about four attributes from the textbook that described them and
explained how those things led them to choose the career path they
had in mind. I, on the other hand, chose to approach the project in
my own, creative way.

When it was my turn, I went to the front of the class and started
writing big letters across the board.

F-E-A-R-L-E-S-S

"Hello, everyone. My name is Jenna, and I am fearless."

I drew a line in between the words fear and less. Fearless was an
acronym that I wrote out like an acrostic poem on the board for the
attributes from the textbook that I felt matched who I was. The F. E.
A. R. letters in the acrostic described attributes of who I was before
the accident. My vocational life plan before the accident was born
out of choosing a safe career path that would cancel out any fears of
not being able to provide for myself. The L. E. S. S. described who I
was after the accident. Even though I was now "less" by many mea-
sures, stepping into my new life and being forced to become a different person had actually turned my fear into fearless.

I explained how I felt exposed and had lost all my labels. Yet, somehow, through my relationship with Christ (which is not talked about

at a New Jersey state school ever), I was far less insecure and fearful about myself now than I was even before the accident. I explained I didn't know how this would translate to what I would do in my career even though I always had a plan for my life and career before the accident.

I shared that being fearless does not mean there is no reason to fear, but rather in spite of fear, I had full faith that God would lead me and provide in each moment, as that moment happens. I believed he would provide for my physical needs, yes, but also my need for purpose and hope here on earth. This was despite having lost everything I would need to answer the questions to complete this presentation as the other students had done. I had no thought-out plan for my vocational goals because I was no longer the one who is writing my story. I would graduate and I would have a vocation, but God was in charge of my timeline. I had plenty of reasons to fear, but I stood there in front of my classmates without any.

When I finished, there was silence. The usual sound of the slow clapping from college students who had listened to only about ten percent of the presentation was absent, as everyone sat completely still. Some of the students even had their mouths open. No one expected me with my bright red lipstick and Instagram smile to get up there and have a presentation like that. I was living in a shell that blinded people from seeing what life was truly like.

Never once did my fellow students imagine I was leaving class to throw up when I went on frequent bathroom breaks from class. Each semester a student from each of my classes was chosen to be a note-taker for a student registered in the Office of Special Services, and I bet they never would have guessed it was me.

Shaking, I went to erase the board and grab my papers as the presentation was now open to the class for questions. I felt confident and at peace, even though I had just totally exposed my biggest insecurities and vulnerabilities in front of all these people. A few years prior, I hadn't wanted to be on earth anymore because I didn't want to answer the questions I had to share in the presentation. But in that moment, I exposed my weaknesses to a bunch of strangers and still felt confident peace. I knew I was worthy of love. I knew I was enough for whatever God had ahead.

I surprised myself during the Fearless presentation because for the first time in my life, I really felt that way. I was nothing other than a Child of God and I knew God gave me my story and platform for a reason. Perhaps what I said could possibly lead someone closer to Him, even if the professor hated it. I had confidence at my lowest, and I wanted that for others too.

I knew this radical transformation was nothing short of a miracle, and I was so happy to share it if it meant that God would lead someone to Him and transform them as well.

My professor let out a loud chuckle and said, "I would hate to be the person presenting after that one. Wow. That was incredible."

As I sat back down at my seat, I almost had to leave class because I was feeling so sick. My nervous system made my body shake while it tried to process all that just happened, but my soul was at peace.

My earthly resume had been a shield that guarded me from worrying about my future vocation, future family, and how others would see or judge me. As much as I needed these resume points to appear successful to others, they had wrongly become the foundation of my own self-esteem, and therefore, my identity.

I find the messaging of our world will tell you to take on only the positive labels. You are an athlete! You are a student! You are a mother! You have an amazing physique! You have an awesome job! These are good things. Focus on the positive. The bad labels don't define you; the good labels do.

It seems like Christians, on the other hand, will tell you to take on more abstract labels instead. You are so giving! You are such a great friend! You are such an encourager! You are a great listener! These labels place your identity in how you do things instead of what you do.

None of these labels worked for me anymore. After the accident, all of the labels I could possibly think of, either physical or abstract, necessitated that I was actually able to do something, and I could do next to nothing. These noun labels relied on their verb forms to back them up.

I had cried out to God: "Please give me my new labels!" I tried to listen intently to the Holy Spirit to see if I could discern a Bible verse or word to cling on to.

God gave me *one* label and *one* label only to tell me who I was: "Child of God." It was almost an audible voice I heard as I remained seated and prayed.

At first, I thought, *OK... 'Child of God'... AND...* I waited patiently in the presence of God for some time. I sat and thought, *OK, He will give me something else, I just know it.* But He didn't.

I did not think only being a Child of God was enough for me, I thought I needed more. How could that one label really and truly be enough for my full source of identity?

No matter who I was now or what I would become, that one label was going to keep me from drowning. It became the foundation I stood upon.

The Child of God label did something I was unaware of, even at the time. Instead of seeing myself and my circumstances when I thought of my identity, I saw God. I saw myself on His team, not Him on my team. I was no longer pointing people to me; I was pointing them to God. I was no longer inviting people to see my resume; I was pointing them to the infinite God of creation. I became a steward rather than an owner.

Investigating my new singular label, a truth laid firm in my heart: everything I had worked for was taken away, but everything God had done in me remained intact.

How could that be? The only thing I had kept when everything fell apart was my faith.

Hebrews 11:1 describes faith: "Now faith is confidence in what we hope for and assurance about what we do not see."

In contrast to the earthly resume I thought I needed, Hebrews Chapter 11 goes on to describe the sort of spiritual resumes that God asks of us. The "resume chapter," as I like to call it, details the lives of famous heroes in the Old Testament all the way to unknown, unnamed martyrs in the New Testament. They all possessed one thing: faith.

This came with a caution. Success from the perspective of God's purposes does not always line up with earthly success. Will I gain favor again in the eyes of those around me? Perhaps. Maybe I would have a story like that of Daniel or Joseph, who overcame trials to become great leaders in the surrounding culture. But what if it was the opposite? What if I lead a life of martyrdom, suffering for the sake of faith?

The "resume chapter" in Hebrews showed me that my suffering on earth was not in vain. Success in the kingdom of God can look like earthly success, or earthly failure. As long as I use my life for God, the earthly results do not determine my status in God's kingdom. Sure, my current suffering was not because of my faith. However, I felt like I was suffering *for the sake of* my faith, by remaining on earth to do His work even though I didn't know what it would look like.

I used to think that the declaration in Philippians 4:13 (NKJV), "I can do all things through Christ who gives me strength," was about setting a goal and reaching it with God's help. I now see that it means that God gives us strength to stay strong in faith no matter the circumstance.

Everything on earth is temporary and I felt that more than ever. Identity in God provides a firm foundation that does not waiver like the labels we have on earth, and that changed the game for me. My resume of faith was growing, even if many times God and I were the only ones who saw it happen.

Only people who undergo some traumatic circumstances lose all of their identity at once, but everyone loses one or two labels at a time as seasons change. Most people try to fill in the gaps with other labels to cover what becomes exposed when a particular piece of identity falls away, but inevitably death erases all labels. What do we do then?

The Christian faith tells us that death isn't the end of our story. There is an eternal significance to what happens during our life on earth. The one, solid label, "Child of God," is a label that will stick with us from this life to the next as an eternal foundation.

Jesus talks about foundations in a parable found in the book of Matthew.

> Therefore everyone who hears these words of mine and puts them into practice is like a wise man who built his house on the rock. The rain came down, the streams rose, and the winds blew and beat against that house; yet it did not fall, because it had its foundation on the rock. But everyone who hears these words of mine and does not put them into practice is like a foolish man who built his house on sand. The rain came down, the streams rose, and the winds blew and beat against that house, and it fell with a great crash (Matthew 7: 24-27).

I believe that parable could be talking about our identity. If it is spiritually built on the things of God that will last from this life until the next, we will not be uprooted in the storms of life. If our identities are built on the sand of earthly success, they could disappear in a moment. What is the rock? Various times in the Bible we see that Christ is the rock on which we stand. I wanted the foundation of my identity to be so strong that the waves of the earth would be no match for my hope and faith in Him.

Before that night looking out over the lake, when I had no hope left in my heart; I was like the foolish man who had built his identity upon the sand. The floodwaters came and I was almost completely destroyed, save for the faith in my heart. The house I lived in, the house of my dreams and plans, was gone. Everything inside of me was emptied, and Christ filled all of the cracks.

Although the facts of my accident and my situation rocked me, my foundation was firm in *The* Rock.

As I watched each person get up and share all the impressive things they would do with their futures in my class, I was shocked that I could be satisfied with the empty, earthly resume I had. I was living counter-culturally to the world and being brought farther and farther out to sea.

Chapter 16

HOW DO YOU HAVE HOPE?

As my spiritual growth progressed, there was very little physical improvement no matter how many doctors we saw.

A neck surgeon specialist who examined my neck suggested spine surgery to address the intense pain. A top NeuroENT surgeon suggested inner ear surgery because he believed that could help my vestibular system and ease the dizziness. Gastroenterologists told me that if I kept puking, my esophagus could fully erode from the stomach acids until it could be completely gone. A top orthopedic surgeon examined my back and told me I had two herniated discs but he couldn't do anything about the pain because pain is all "in the mind."

Another orthopedic doctor was alarmed by how bad my neck and back were, but he was out of options for me as I had already gone through years of failed physical therapy. He told me that the only thing I could do was to sit in the pain with prescription ibuprofen. We explored every area of my health that we could imagine, including some diets and holistic approaches. For every doctor that suggested surgery, there was another doctor who said surgery would be taking too great a risk given my fragile condition, potentially leaving me so much worse than I already was.

This even extended to my friendly dentist, who gave a grave report about how the stomach acids were eroding my teeth. I was so young and had "my whole life ahead of me," he told me as he gave me special toothpaste to attempt to slow the erosion.

One constant throughout this multi-year season of different doctors and treatments was vision therapy. I was determined to work my way through what I thought was the root cause of my issues.

One day I went into vision therapy for what seemed like the thousandth time. It was a diagnostic day, which meant I had to get through all the parts of the testing no matter what. On these days I would usually throw up before we even made it to the part of the appointment where the doctor came into the room. I would not be able to do much actual vision therapy on diagnostic days, which was frustrating because I was already so behind schedule for how people normally progressed.

This diagnostic day was centered around a new comprehension evaluation. I would read a few pages of a book to myself while wearing specialized goggles that tracked what my eyes were doing. I wasn't allowed to read out loud so that they could test only my visual reading and memory. The vision tracking would show how long I spent on a word or phrase and if I was going back and re-reading parts of it. At the end, they would ask comprehension questions to determine my reading level—something no one knew at the time. A high school reading level would be embarrassing, and a middle school level would be mortifying. I was apprehensive and afraid my comprehension may have regressed since I had been able to read for only a few minutes at a time for years now.

I took a deep breath, and I started reading. I kept reading a phrase which made no sense to me. I was having a difficult time and Luli (my vision therapist) saw quickly and decided to give me an easier book.

She made up some sort of excuse so I wasn't embarrassed and gave me a children's book instead. I felt better because surely, I could read this book. I would at least be able to follow what the words were saying.

I tried to read each sentence and remember what I was reading. Simultaneously, each time I tried to think hard, the room would start to spin, and my eyes would get blurry or go into double vision. It was so tough because after each sentence, my mind would go blank. I would have no idea what I just read, but I kept going. I smiled, cracked a joke, and did all I could not to throw up. I did my best. I sought out different words I imagined were important and tried to remember one word per sentence so I could get the questions correct at the end.

It was a mess. My vision therapist took off my testing goggles and unplugged the wires. She began to ask me questions that were super hard. I thought they must have been trick questions because I wasn't remembering any of the answers, and the children's book I was reading had only a few sentences per cardboard page.

I didn't realize it at the time, but this test was especially hard for me because it singled out my visual memory. My visual memory was so bad that I would forget the words as soon as I stopped looking at the page. I could have looked back through the book and found the answer, but if I wasn't looking at it, the information was gone. For schoolwork, I could retain a little more because I heard the words by reading it out loud or from a recording on theMP3 player, as per my accommodations. Something about hearing made it possible for me to retain certain parts of what I read, but this test was solely visual.

"How did I do?" I took a deep breath once again.

The therapist looked at me and squinted as if she were wincing in pain. She shifted in her seat. "Well…"

First grade. I had a first-grade reading level.

I looked at my mom as I welled up with tears. Her eyes were also filled with tears, but she pushed them back and gave me a nod of reassurance.

I couldn't even read a children's book and understand it. No wonder school was so difficult. I now understood why I could barely take one or two classes at a time even after several semesters at my new school.

I began to pray. I prayed God would meet me there. I thanked Him that my hope was not in my ability. I thanked God that He could not love me any more or less than He did right then. I thanked Him that I had purpose even though I had such limited ability. I thanked Him for that very moment and that He would be with me in all my future moments.

Years before, I would've seen this trial as my own failure and believed no one could love a failure like me. That day I sat somewhat numb, yet fully grounded. My worth was not in what I could do, and good thing, because it sure looked like I could do next to nothing. A college student who couldn't read…

It was one of those shocking moments of being slapped with reality. There was no denying or escaping how bad I was. It was not theoretical. It was hard science, right in front of us.

But God would not ask me to have purpose beyond my abilities, and He would find purpose in my inability. Thanking God and affirming that He was in control was like a highway to hope.

The office staff gave me a few minutes to recover my vision and stability, and we headed in to see Dr. Mark. My mom and I really liked Dr. Mark. He was the doctor under the man who owned the practice, and we appreciated how personable he was.

I sat down in the big chair. I prayed God would continue to use me even though they were telling me haunting things. Soon, Dr. Mark came into the room and greeted my mother and me.

"Hey Dr. Mark, how's it going?" I said with a big smile as I laughed a little bit. We all knew we were in for some tough conversations, so I decided to try and break it up a little bit. He laughed quietly to himself with a nervous smile as he sat down.

He explained some of my symptoms and diagnostic results. On top of the reading level issue, I had progressed only a minuscule amount, which was not normal. The walls of the office were filled with success stories, pictures of past patients that smiled at you as you walked down the hallway. They had come in once a week or more for a few weeks or months. I, on the other hand, had been coming in for a double session twice a week for multiple years.

Dr. Mark talked about other potential treatment options for my other non-visual symptoms, but he offered no clear path for my recovery, especially when it came to vision therapy. This was rather shocking to my mom and me. I don't remember exactly what he said, but he was clearly very sad and had little hope I would get any better. I fixed my mind on the hope Jesus had given me to keep my spirits up. I did not want to break down and cry.

For years, Dr. Mark had been the one who encouraged us to move forward with vision therapy. He was the one who was giving us hope for my recovery. He would show us that I had moved forward only an inch on the charts (and had about five feet to go), but an inch was something!

Now things were different. He took me through the doctor version of a break-up and seemingly rescinded all of his past hopeful comments about my recovery. He was not going to continue to make me throw up doing their exercises for progress that was almost too small to measure.

It was my turn to respond, but what could I say? He half listened to me as I searched for the right words. I decided to share about the purposes God was giving me amidst my inability. It was probably more for me than for him.

Dr. Mark stopped in his tracks. He sat down and looked me in the eyes and calmly questioned, "Jenna, how could you possibly have hope?" He was leveling with me as a friend.

I took a deep breath. "Well… How could I not?"

I told him my hope is secure. It is not dependent on what happens today or who looks like they are winning. My hope is in the one who will wipe every tear from our eyes. Revelation 21:4 says, "He will wipe every tear from their eyes. There will be no more death or mourning or crying or pain, for the old order of things has passed away."

Dr. Mark watched me carefully as I spoke, considering each of my words and their impact. I continued speaking, confident in the truth that flowed out of my mouth. After all, hope was the thing keeping me together the most.

The new me had truly experienced first-hand, complete reliance on God to be my only source of self-worth. God was so real to me that every promise in the Bible rang true in my heart in a new way. There was so much hope, even if I would barely be able to read the rest of my life. There was no doubt in my mind that God was with me. I had no fear that He was going to leave me stranded. I had more hope than ever knowing God was going to come through as He says He will.

Hope was not just something in my head; it was a part of me. It became something people could see on my face no matter how poorly I was doing physically.

In the dark examination room, Dr. Mark looked at me with an even more serious face than ever before. With tears in his eyes he finally spoke: "It's people with faith like yours who change the world."

We sat in a moment of silence. I pursed my lips together in a pleasant half-smile to acknowledge him without having to speak. He eventually turned around to his desk and moved some papers as silence still filled the room. My half-smile turned into a chuckle. I didn't know how a college girl sitting in a therapy room, unable to read or comprehend a children's book, could change the world. But more importantly, I was no longer striving to do so. I was happy to be my small behind-the-scenes part of the body of Christ, knowing that God Himself has and will change the world.

Being let go from vision therapy was a day that would stand out to my mother and me in infamy. After years of such hard work, I wasn't really any better, and they didn't have any real guidance for what I should do moving forward. It felt like vision therapy had robbed me of years of my life. All those times I puked were for nothing. All the physical pain I went through in my eyes, head, and neck was now for nothing. All the money we spent—gone. All of the time we could have spent on another treatment that might have actually worked was gone too. We trusted these people. We trusted God that this was the right step at the time. It seemed so promising...

I welled up with tears, not for lack of hope but for sadness for my body. I had put so much work into the tests and had lost so many hours to exacerbated symptoms due to therapy.

Just like a movie, it was an ominous, rainy day as we left their offices for the last time.

The rain beat down on our car as tears rained slowly down my mother's and my faces. Because I felt so full of the presence of God, I could not bring myself to sob. The tears were slow. I should have been devastated, but I wasn't. These tears came from self-compassion instead of self-loathing.

I took a deep breath and told myself that the experience of vision therapy was not a waste. Just like on my last day, I had brought Jesus into that space for years. I had spoken up when I felt prompted, and I knew some of my conversations about God had moved people. Hope accompanied me each time I walked in. The therapists had become my friends, and the doctor was like an older brother. They saw I was suffering, but I was also being filled each and every day with a purpose beyond my ability.

I felt one with Christ in suffering, as I remained alive for Him.

Chapter 17

STILL SMALL VOICE

She knew the sun would set,
Yet the color still surprised her.
How beautiful it was, but yet,
Her part in it was but a blur.

The sun was moving on,
As were the clouds she knew.
But there is promise in the dawn,
Not where the birds once flew.

She remembered how the rain,
Is always replaced by sun.
That even in her pain,
Her story is not done.

And when the dawn appears,
And all the colors fade,
The answers will be clear,
To all the prayers she prayed.

mourned the day my friends graduated from my first college. It was sad that they were moving on. It was sad that I never got to go back. I still had such a long way to go for my own graduation. I opened Instagram and saw their graduation caps bedazzled with "Jeremiah 29:11: 'For I know the plans I have for you,' says the Lord. 'Plans to prosper you and not to harm you. Plans to give you a hope and a future.'" I believed that verse with all of my heart, but it seemed easier to say when you just graduated with honors from your dream school than when you are struggling through one or two classes a semester.

While I was crawling through at a snail's pace, it was impossible to know how I would make it through required classes, like Business Technology, a fully computer-based class for freshmen that I had been avoiding for obvious reasons. I also dreaded Math 101 because it required a convoluted computerized placement exam that was timed and that changed after each question based on whether you got it right or wrong. This kind of exam was not easily transferable to pen and paper, which is what I would have needed to survive more than a few questions.

After a few upper-level accounting courses, I started to seriously reevaluate whether sticking with accounting was the right thing to do, even after all this time. The occupational therapist didn't exactly give me a suitable alternative, so I hadn't changed my major as of yet.

I knew God wanted me to be at school, even though it was such a tough thing to put my body through. It was confusing, but I knew I had to stay. I felt like God was asking me: "Will you keep going, even though it's hard?"

A common misconception I sort of believed was that plans ordained by God would work out easily while plans not ordained by God would be filled with roadblocks. I no longer believed that. Doors, whether open or shut, felt difficult and hard to navigate.

People were praying for me, and one person even told me to go out and buy a briefcase because we were going to trust that God would bring me through this injury to success and completion. I wanted to believe that more than anything, but I could tell that God was bringing me to a different place.

I didn't buy a briefcase for my future accounting job, believing it would happen. Through everything I was learning about my body and what God had for me, I felt I needed to do something different. It was time for me to officially change my major. I had to face the facts. Reading small numbers, concentrating through difficult problem-solving, and looking intently at spreadsheets on the computer was no longer an option for me. Why should I have a degree in a field for which I physically cannot do the work?

I stood in the Center for Student Success looking at the forms for quite some time. I even had a hard time reading which one I had to grab to change my major. I felt the still, small voice of God telling me that He was with me if I really wanted to continue with school. If I wanted to continue to give classes my all, He would be by my side supporting me. He was holding back my hair and shedding a tear as I puked in the bathroom stalls. He was the one that orchestrated the A's I would get between memory lapses. It clearly was not on my own. I felt a promise that God would show up in each moment. Not early, not late, but right on time, each time.

"Business Administration with a concentration in Marketing." I circled my new major on the form. It was the obvious choice. All of the classes I had already taken would count toward business administration, and marketing was the least small-numbers intensive of the other concentrations, yet with its own challenges all the same.

I still would have to take the required classes I was putting off, but that semester I found some of my new classes to be fascinating and a much better fit. I started to love marketing and began to talk about it all the time.

I could not help the nagging notion that it wasn't the major I had always wanted, but I felt the Lord reassuring me in each small step.

Since I had also moved on from all of the therapies at the time, it was time to find something else. My mom was determined to help me improve and would not take no for an answer.

I felt like I was in a holding pattern. Everyone else's life was changing, but mine was staying the same. None of them were caught in the deep waves I still lost my breath in.

With nowhere to go and no idea what to do next, my mom once again scoured the internet for doctors who could help me: books, blogs, websites, anything and everything she could find on traumatic brain injuries, concussions, contusions, and post-traumatic rehabilitation.

She came across a book written by a professor of artificial intelligence who meticulously documented his own experience with a concussion and subsequent many years of failed therapies. He was later immensely helped by a team of doctors in Chicago, many years after the supposed recovery window was over. A lot of his issues were the same as mine and a lot of them were not. We learned more about the doctors and their patients—lawyers, accountants, high-level athletes, professors, doctors, and other high achievers—who were able to get back to their old lives for the most part after treatment.

When we spoke with the doctors, we could tell they were so different from the doctors I had been seeing. They wanted to mold a recovery track unique to me rather than try to fit me into a standard recovery process. Plus, they believed there were solutions that could help me, emphasizing that the brain can rewire itself and learn new ways to do things no matter how much time has passed.

We felt like they were a great fit, but we did not want to go to Chicago. We would go all the way out there, only for them to say they couldn't help me when they saw me fall down or throw up. Why would this be different from any of the other doctor's we had been to?

The discouragement in our hearts hung low, but we were desperate because my quality of life was so low. The memory lapse issues bothered my parents more than they let on, and my lack of mental endurance was almost just as concerning. Holidays were getting more and more disappointing. Christmas, Thanksgiving, Easter, birthdays,

Fourth of July, Labor Day, weddings, vacations, and all sorts of other happy events were being continually overshadowed by my intense symptoms. I was accidentally ruining countless happy times by throwing up violently or falling down. I didn't want to be the main family topic anymore. I didn't want to ruin plans, and I didn't want to be involved in plans either. It was not something we could just live with. We had to find answers.

My family discussed thoroughly whether we should go to Chicago or not. First off, traveling is expensive. Secondly, we were all exhausted after four years of trying every doctor and therapy we could possibly find. Did we have the energy to fully commit to this new approach to therapy? Would this really turn out differently? We kept asking God what to do. We prayed for wisdom. Friends, family, and our church prayed for wisdom for us, too.

Saying yes when it's a clear-cut act of faith in God seemed simpler than this. Leading the Christian fellowship at school or creating designs at J. Shotmeyer were obviously good things. But what about problems that don't seem to have an easy answer?

We believe that God gives direction for even non-spiritual things, if we ask (and more importantly, listen). God was asking not only me, but our family: "Will you listen to my still, small voice?"

Discussing it one day, my mom opened her Bible and told us that when she was asking God what to do, she kept thinking of Naaman. She did not fully remember Naaman's story in the Old Testament, and she looked it up. Naaman was a foreign man with leprosy who was unfamiliar with the Jewish faith, and Elisha was a Jewish prophet in Israel (see 2 Kings 5). Naaman came to Elisha to request that Elisha heal him of his leprosy, expecting Elisha to perform some elaborate ritual. Instead, Elisha simply instructed Naaman to wash seven times in the Jordan River to be healed:

> But Naaman became furious, and went away and said,
> 'Indeed, I said to myself, "He will surely come out *to me*,

and stand and call on the name of the Lord his God, and
wave his hand over the place, and heal the leprosy." Are
not the Abanah and the Pharpar, the rivers of Damascus,
better than all the waters of Israel? Could I not wash in
them and be clean?' So he turned and went away in a rage
(2 Kings 5:11-12 NKJV).

But then Naaman's servants convinced him to follow the instruc-
tion and said to him:

> "My father, if the prophet had told you to do something
> great, would you not have done it? How much more then,
> when he says to you, 'Wash, and be clean?'" (2 Kings 5:13
> NKJV).

Reading that story, my mom finally felt at peace about going to
Chicago. God was directing us to this next step. We did not want
to go to Chicago, just as Naaman did not want to go to the Jordan
river to be healed. We did not know why we needed to go to Chicago when we lived outside of New York City, but we were being
asked to step out.

Saying yes to God in this instance still scared me. It was listening to the small voice that pushed me onward. God had been with
me deeply and intimately as I went to vision therapy every week
for years, and I knew all too well how that had worked out. I trea-
sured the work that I know I did for his Kingdom, but I mourned
my tired and sad body. I knew he was with me now, and I knew that
he wanted me to be better, but that didn't mean that these doctors
would be able to help.

I clung to Romans 12:12: "Therefore, I urge you, brothers and sisters, in view of God's mercy, to offer your bodies as a living sacrifice,
holy and pleasing to God—this is your true and proper worship."

This would be how I would not grow bitter if the doctors were
not able to help. I was a living sacrifice for God. If this plan ended

only in more pain, I would trust that my sacrifice for Christ would be worth it because we were now so certain he was leading us to go there. If it did help me, I would praise God the same as if it didn't help me. Why? Because I was alive only for him. There was a bigger plan going on among us, and my biggest hope was to be faithful with what I had.

I believed with all of my heart that "all things work together for good to those who love God, and are called according to His purpose" (Romans 8:28 NKJV).

I was surely called according to His purpose. As far as all things working for good, I knew I wasn't limited to what I saw on earth. There is a whole eternity for God to shine His goodness. Even if I stayed like this my whole life, I held tightly onto the truth that there is so much good, even if we don't see it until heaven.

When we got to Chicago, we were inspired to find that they saw my symptoms and nausea as motivation for treatment rather than obstacles to treatment. And instead of half-listening and trying to treat me as a cookie-cutter case, they took everything I said into consideration and even asked more questions.

It felt like I had an all-star team at my disposal. One doctor specialized in vision and the way that the eyes communicate with the brain. Another dealt with processing and visual memory through puzzles. Another worked on my body mechanics, and still another focused on diet and supplements to work on my recovery chemically. It was so interesting to talk with these brilliant minds who saw my case as a challenging puzzle.

When I got on the plane to leave Chicago, I had a recovery plan that made some sense to me and lots of homework exercises to do. I looked out the window over the clouds.

"Hope on earth is a curious thing," I wrote in the notes section of my phone. "It's exciting, but somehow scary."

If I put my hope and trust in these doctors to make me better, was I not putting my hope in God to heal me?

I began to think about the lyrics of a popular Christian song: "Even if you don't, my hope is you alone." Now it seemed like, "even if God does help me feel better through doctors, my hope is still in Him alone."

I was so fascinated with the doctors' work and my treatments. The vision doctor prescribed special glasses that targeted which neuroreceptors in the eye receive light, a technique that affected much more than just vision and was the critical piece described in extreme detail in the book my mom had read. I found that the glasses profoundly affected my spatial orientation, sometimes making me sick or fall down, so I was especially careful going up and down stairs. The cognitive specialist prescribed puzzles that affected me in equally strange ways. After completing a few puzzles, I would sometimes collapse after getting up from my desk, even when I felt like I hadn't done too many. Other times, I found myself walking directly into walls and not knowing why. But I would eventually adjust to the glasses setup and recover from the strange mental overload from the puzzles and be a little bit better than before, and the doctors actually liked that my nervous system was responding to them.

Thankfully, we were able to keep up with the vision doctor because she saw patients one or two days a month in Brooklyn, NY. The cognitive specialist also worked out of Florida, and so we were able to coordinate my visits with my father's business trips.

A year in, one of the doctors from the team was discouraged with my progress, but the most brilliant of them all just laughed and said, "Jenna is not a quick-fix situation."

That year of puzzles and glasses was a long and difficult one, to say the least, and I had not seen any of the relatively quick-fix prognoses that others had. I was using the glasses (which were adjusted every few months or so) and doing religiously what each doctor had said. I became able to drive across town in the middle of the day when I felt the best. Sure, I could not go to the busy grocery store, which would be an intense sensory overload, but I could sometimes drive to my school, rest, go to class, and then sleep for a while and maybe even drive home. It was a huge feat, but still a far cry from the radical change I would need to live independently or have full-time career options again.

There always seemed to be something impeding my progress. My vision was too bad for my vestibular system to get the help it needed. My vestibular system was too bad for my neck, back and body to get the help they needed. My neck and back were too bad for me to get the vision help I needed, and it all spiraled over and over and over. With these new doctors, something had to give in order to achieve a breakthrough.

I was still just as nauseous, just as weak, just as tired.

In the depths of January in 2018, I went to Canada with my family. After the long car ride, I looked out on the river in Quebec City that was almost totally frozen over. The ice on the river would move ever so slightly, and similar to being at a stoplight when the car next to you rolls forward, my body didn't know whether I was moving or if my surroundings were moving. I instantly became nauseous and uneasy, and we made our way back into the hotel. Suddenly, I collapsed right there in the lobby, so dizzy I could not get up. Everyone rushed to me in their huge jackets, gloves, and hats, but I was unable to stand. I tried again but couldn't get up. The room felt like it was moving so fast, and I was stuck on the floor. I was embarrassed, so I kept trying with all that I had to stop making a scene. I laid there looking at the ceiling, unable to move, trapped in my body.

What started out as a great idea for a fun trip ended with me staying in bed for most of it. We were supposed to have lots of quality time together as a family, but I had to beg them to go out and do things without me.

Soon after, in the beginning of 2018, I began to back out of everything. Not to isolate myself, but to take care of myself. I tried to hear the voice of God, but in its still, small quiet, it was difficult.

How many times would I let myself collapse before I get really hurt? How many times would I go somewhere knowing it would probably make me puke?

The first four and a half years after the accident, I needed to socially get out and still do things. I did not want to miss out on life events and fun. Now, I felt more mature and needed to make decisions that would be sustainable for me long-term. I wasn't depressed; I was much more confident than I had been before. My hope was secure, but my body felt weaker and weaker, still being carried out to sea by the riptide.

Chapter 18

WILL YOU SHOW UP?

I was being beaten by waves of discouragement and so much physical pain as March of 2018 rolled around.

I had wrestled for weeks about going to the two-day women's conference at my church. I absolutely loved my church, but ever since the accident, my nervous system could not handle the lights and loud music. Wearing earplugs, sunglasses, and sitting in the back row was not enough for me to make it through a Sunday without throwing up and being completely shot for the rest of the day. Sometimes, I would sit in the foyer, not even going into the sanctuary and *still* get sick. So, I finally started giving myself a break, staying home on Sundays and watching the service online more often, but it wasn't the same. I reminded myself of the nurse that told me that I needed to stop throwing up to prevent irreversible damage to my throat and esophagus. I sure hated the sound of that.

On top of that, I was slated to introduce my grandfather immediately after the conference ended at a black-tie event hosted by my college. It's not every day that your grandfather gets honored by your school, so of course I agreed to speak for a couple of minutes and stumble back to my car. Could I afford to attend a two-day conference before that, though? The answer was no…

But this was the women's conference, one of the most special times for me and the fellow women of my church to freely seek God and worship together. Plus, Jacob and I had created custom J. Shotmeyer journals specially for the conference. They were pink with gold letters which said "Flourish," as that was the conference's theme. When you opened the pink journal, there was a sunflower pattern, which was explained in a write-up within each notebook:

There is a lot we can learn from sunflowers.

As sunflowers grow, they open their faces towards the sun. When we turn our faces to the sun, the darkness casts its shadow behind us. Although the sun is always present, it cannot shine on us if we are turned away. We need the sun in order to thrive because we cannot live without light. Just like flowers need the sunlight, we need God's light through His son to flourish and grow. We look toward the light through thankfulness and worship to truly flourish.

The bees in the pattern represent the Holy Spirit because we thrive through His pollination and truth. He buzzes all around us, providing peace as we allow Him to move in us.

The pink paint splotches are God's beauty sprinkled throughout our lives. Through Christ's nourishment, we will not only flourish and grow but we will see sprinkles of God's beauty and blessing no matter our circumstances. God's beauty is both in the seen and unseen realms. It will be shown to us as we seek His face, allowing the Holy Spirit to pollinate our hearts.

Lastly, sunflowers grow together in great volumes. Often, there are fields of sunflowers that are all growing in close proximity

*to each other. As those who are seeking the Son, we are called
to commune and grow with our brothers and sisters in Christ.*

I wanted to go to the conference so badly, but I didn't want to puke
at church again. I didn't want to sit in the hallway and have everyone ask me if I was OK. I couldn't physically sit inside the sanctuary
up front where I would love to be. I was perplexed.

With these thoughts swirling in my head, I headed to my school's
gym after class. I had started doing five- to ten-minute stationary
bike sessions that semester, which I was really enjoying. If the ground
moved under my feet during one of my workouts, the sturdiness of
the bike helped me keep my balance so I didn't fall. But I had to be
careful to not exceed those five to ten minutes because I may not have
been able to walk back from the gym if I did more.

I climbed on a bike and paused to decide whether to put on an
uplifting podcast or an episode of *Gilmore Girls*. I admittedly had
spent more time on Netflix than I had in my Bible recently, but this
time I decided on a podcast by a preacher from northern California.
It was a week before our women's conference, and I will never forget
his perspective on spiritual gifts. He said that each of us have spiritual gifts that others need, and others have spiritual gifts that we need.
That is why we go to church. We need community to fully enter into
what God wants for us.

His message was about showing up. Sometimes, he said, you need
to show up to receive from God. God is outstretching His hand, and
we need to get together and show up to walk in the destiny God has
prepared for us.

I knew in an instant that God was asking me to go to the conference, and I made a commitment that I would show up. Perhaps
God could give me even just an ounce of something to lift me up. I
needed something, because I was struggling emotionally, physically,

and spiritually, and I was discouraged with my recovery. While the Chicago doctors still seemed like they were helping to some extent, my improvement was slower than we all hoped. It seemed likely that my favorite doctor who came to Brooklyn would discharge me because my progress with her glasses had slowed to a crawl. Those around me were running out of hope again for earthly recovery.

What about God, "The Great Physician"? I thought to myself.

I believed God could heal me, but by this point I didn't pray for that very often. Matt prayed for me and my recovery every night on the phone, but he would usually pray for a reprieve from symptoms, like nausea, or that I wouldn't get sick if I was going somewhere the next day. Every now and then we would pray for full-on miraculous healing, but those times became fewer and farther between as the years dragged on. It was just too painful to get emotionally invested in something that wasn't happening, and praying for full freedom and release from the injury had sometimes made me unable to see God's purpose for me in the midst of that life situation.

The times I let myself pray for my full healing had been somewhat painful. I thought back to one of those times a year before at my church. While I was crouched in the back with my earplugs and sunglasses, the speaker started to pray that God would heal His people. I started weeping on my knees in the back row, hands lifted high, crying out, "Jesus, don't pass me by! Please don't pass me by! Jesus, please!"

I probably cried out for ten or twenty minutes just like that and nothing happened.

I felt like Jesus *had* passed me by. I knew in my heart that He loved me, and I knew He was with me, but for whatever reason He didn't heal me. Of course, I had prayed many times before to be healed, and He hadn't healed me those times either.

Six months before the women's conference, I found myself in a similar situation. I was home alone, very sad that I was unable to attend the Thanksgiving Eve service at my church. I turned on a livestream from a very dynamic church, and they just happened to have a half hour set aside exclusively for praying for healing from head trauma. I really thought this was my moment. I was in my bed, home alone, wailing out to my Father in heaven asking Him to take this injury from me, but He didn't.

It was difficult to pray for my healing and still value what God was doing through my pain. Somehow, believing I could be healed meant longing for a future me that looked radically different, and it was too hard and too painful for me to pray for that every day.

It reminded me of a passage in the Bible. In Matthew 11, John the Baptist, who was Jesus' cousin and the one who "prepared the way for the Lord," was in jail. He sent his disciples to Jesus and asked if Jesus is really who He says He is. John's whole life had been dedicated to declaring Jesus as the Son of God, yet he sat in jail and asked this question. Jesus did not save John from jail, but responded to the disciples, "Go back and report to John what you hear and see: The blind receive sight, the lame walk, those who have leprosy are cleansed, the deaf hear, the dead are raised, and the good news is proclaimed to the poor. Blessed is anyone who does not stumble on account of me" (Matthew 11:4-6).

Jesus was doing miracles everywhere, but did not save John from jail. I trusted and welcomed the mystery of Jesus. I was OK, even in intense pain. He could come through and take my physical pain away right then, but He hadn't, and I was at peace knowing I was supposed to trust this mystery.

This was all difficult for me to wrap my clouded mind around, but I still felt so much peace in the presence of Jesus. He was with me everywhere I went. I knew He wasn't passing me by, even when He didn't heal me. He was inside of me, giving me hope, truth, and love. God had so much purpose in my struggles, as I had learned for almost five years. But it was also important for me to remember that although there was so much purpose in my pain, God was not happy I was suffering. I felt like God was crying with me while I would cry myself to sleep. I felt like He was sad with me as I looked up from puking in New York City bathrooms with tears streaming down my face. This wasn't a cruel test He was putting me through—He journeyed with me in my pain.

We live in a broken world, and that hurts God so much that He sent His son to be broken with us and for us. His life lived and laid down brings more love to the world than anything else we have ever seen or experienced. Just as God restored Jesus to life, God promises to restore the earth and wipe every tear from our eyes. The battle is already won.

I knew that Jesus *did* answer my prayers to be healed. In heaven, my pain will be gone. I will have a new body, one that is not full of this pain. God answers all of my prayers for healing as His daughter; I just may not see it on this side of heaven.

I was hoping to be reminded of some of these truths at the conference as I quickly got ready and headed to the church Friday evening. I just wanted to trade some discouragement for hope and get back to my bed that night without throwing up. I was in the lobby of the foyer passing out journals, and women were talking and walking every which way. I was hardly able to listen to any songs or to the speaker, and I ended up puking in the parking lot when it was time to leave. I left church that night encouraged spiritually and discouraged physically.

I went to bed and planned to rest all the next day so that I could function enough to introduce my grandfather at night. Matt, who was at a research conference in California, was understandably concerned about me and all of the events I had packed into the weekend. My whole family knew I couldn't (or shouldn't) do that much, but we also didn't want to stand in the way of God moving.

At eleven the next morning, I laid in bed as the room spun. I thought about how I would rally myself to be productive that day. I reached for my phone and refreshed my emails. My newest email was from Gap. A jumpsuit I ordered just under forty-eight hours ago had arrived.

How could it be here already? I thought as my eyes strained to read small parts of the email. It was the perfect thing to wear to the conference. I smiled because it felt like God was calling me to go back. But how could I, in my right mind, go back to the conference?

I took a deep breath and went to the mailbox, brought it inside, and tried it on. To my amazement, it fit *and* I really liked it. Jumpsuits never looked quite right on me, so I was amazed by the fact that it fit well.

I smiled up at God that He would use a jumpsuit that fit just right to show me I needed to go back to the conference. Still, my stomach turned as I imagined putting myself through more pain.

I grabbed my jean jacket and called my dad to ask for a ride to church. I had missed the morning service, but there was an afternoon prayer service I could just make. The session would be an hour long, followed by another session at night. I promised myself I would just stay for the hour and then have my dad pick me back up.

I walked in yet again to the packed church service with sunglasses and earplugs. I was in so much pain that I did not even sit in the last row. Rather, I sat my back against the wall of the sanctuary, crouched down behind the pews with my head between my knees so that I would not have to see any lights. *Why do I keep doing this to myself?*

The speaker began to prophesy and pray over specific people. Before I knew it, he asked if anyone's father's name was Charles, but more specifically, Chuck. My father's name.

I did my best to come to my feet and saw my sister standing in the front row. I desperately wanted to be with her for this moment. I called to her with no avail, thinking she could meet me in the middle. Hundreds of people were looking for the "daughters of Chuck" as he asked again if anyone fit that description.

I bit the bullet, holding the walls in the dark sanctuary with my head low to the ground as I slowly made my way to my sister. She stood up and I took her seat to stay steady and tucked my head away between my knees again to protect myself from all that was around me.

The speaker began to say that God was going to "show up and show off" in our circumstance. He said that what "the enemy planned for evil, God will turn to good." He said that "encounters are coming."

He did not know my sister or me. He had not heard what had happened to me. Prompted by his prophecy, the whole church prayed for us for a few minutes, and then I slipped out the side door and escaped to a private place.

I was not healed, but I felt the presence of God so strongly.

Chapter 19

DO YOU WANT TO BE HEALED?

There were many times I thought that the riptide could be spitting me out soon. Every wave wasn't a huge wave, but they kept coming. Rocked time and time again, it was obvious when I wasn't spat out. When I walked out of the sanctuary, it was like a calm in the storm, as you see the sun and wonder if you are in the eye of the hurricane or if you are on the other side of it.

I was content to be healed of the toxic thoughts that had wanted to send me to the grave. Sometimes physical healing felt like too much to ask because I already felt so blessed. Being injured was a hard road to walk, but a fulfilling one through the eyes of faith.

A few people came and found me and mentioned they wanted to pray with me, so we went upstairs to a quiet room. At that point, my dad had come to pick me up again, and my brother was on a break from selling merchandise at the conference shop. They walked upstairs to join me, along with my mother and the four or five people who wanted to join me in prayer.

I knew I would have to navigate a delicate balance, protecting myself from hopes that I would be healed that day, while simultaneously waiting in expectancy and full faith. At least God would surely give me some of the encouragement and wisdom I so desperately needed.

As we moved into prayer, I felt God asking me questions.

The first was, "Do you want to be healed?"

Well, *OF COURSE*!!!!!

But in a certain way, it was scary to imagine living in a new body again. Immediately after the accident, I did not know my body at all, and now I had a sense of control in knowing I would forever feel terrible. Control is not a substitute for peace, as each day living in pain was a difficult one.

Trauma reminded my body that the last time my life was changed in a moment, I felt unbelievable pain and disorientation. Being healed would mean no pain, but there would definitely be disorientation, or at least reorientation.

It was also a question of moving on. God was asking me: "Do you trust me in leading a life that you don't know or understand, *again?*"

Being hurt was what I *knew*. It felt like *that* was my purpose here on earth. I felt like I was grounded in my purpose on earth. It was my only constant. I didn't remember high school. I didn't remember what it felt like to live pain-free. Being healed meant every single aspect of my life would change in a moment… again. Would my purpose on earth be gone if a miracle happened?

I remembered the passage in John 5 where Jesus asked this very question: "Do you want to be healed?" to a man who had been disabled for 38 years.

I've heard people say, "Of course he wanted to be healed!" and even insinuate that Jesus could have been being funny or sarcastic.

However, after the years I went through, I would say it is a fair question. For me, I had never heard any pastor or podcaster talk about this in relation to identity before, but I felt that this was Jesus' intention for me at that moment.

Throwing up and feeling terrible was my normal. It was something I tried every day to separate from my identity, but I was constantly labeled by the injury. It is easy to want to grab hold of something when there is pain and trauma. I hated being sick, and in that moment, I knew that I had to mentally separate my identity as a Child of God from the identifier of someone who was so hurt.

Other questions popped up too. How would I tell my doctors about a healing from God, *if* He even chose to heal me? Would they believe me? Would I be labeled as crazy?

One of the worst things about brain injuries is that some people could have thought I was exaggerating symptoms since they couldn't see them. Having an injury that was completely internal had its perks at times, but it was a hard and lonely road to walk. If people don't believe in miracles, wouldn't they just think I had been exaggerating? If I were to be completely healed in that moment, would I lose friends?

I felt the Holy Spirit expose the fears that crept in as a response to God's question of asking me if I wanted to be healed, and I surrendered them over to the Lord, answering, "YES!" I wanted to be healed, and I wanted God to be the one who healed me. I felt God calling me to make the conscious choice to step into that space of full faith and total surrender, but I also knew that truly opening myself up to a miracle meant that I would potentially need to face God saying no again.

God's questions got more specific: "Do you trust me to give you a different purpose?"

Did I *want* that purpose? If God heals me, *that* is my story. I would be a poster child for miracles of healing. My story would not be a "Jesus and…" story. It would be a "Jesus only" story.

Some people wouldn't like that. Some *Christian* people wouldn't like that. I laid those fears aside and told God I would be faithful to walk in whatever purpose He would bring my way.

I continued to pray aloud with those in the room, working through issues that were affecting me at deep emotional and spiritual levels.

We outlined my fears as we prayed, and I saw that those fears contradicted so much of what Jesus came to earth to do. I had to let them go and step into full faith. I wonder if fear is one of the biggest hindrances that keeps us from experiencing miracles today, trapping us in the same painful routines. I do believe that our fears and doubts may be able to hold us back from experiencing miracles at times. But I also believe that the person who is hurt could have no fear and no doubt and still not receive from God what we are asking for. There is so much mystery to the inner working of spiritual things. There were times in the past where I laid down each and every fear, crying out to God and still I was not healed. I put aside that fear knowing it could happen again and entered into expectancy for what God could do.

After a few hours, people understandably had to start leaving. One by one, each person who had prayed for me would give me a hug and walk back downstairs. I didn't know what to think and neither did my parents or brother. I felt drained from a long day of emotions.

But I know this for sure: I walked out of that room maintaining my balance and without a sick sense of nausea for the first time in four and a half years.

There was no opportunity to test out my seemingly new physical condition, process the hours that had just unfolded, jump for joy, or continue crying, because I had a grandfather to introduce. I put on a black gown, reapplied makeup over my tear-stained, puffy face, and went out the door to the event.

I didn't wait in the car at the event as I had planned to; I walked right in. I spoke to people without losing my train of thought. I walked on steady ground. I was not in excruciating pain as the blaring music piped through the room. What a contrast to puking in the bushes just trying to walk to my parents' car twenty-four hours before!

When it came time for me to speak, I got up with peace and poise. It was all a blur, but I must've done a great job because the compliments I received were over the top. I walked through the crowd and someone stopped me every few steps to tell me they were floored with how great my two-minute speech was. I even got invited to apply to multiple jobs at multiple companies. It was one impressed person after another.

I knew it wasn't really me they were impressed with. Something was different. I had just been touched by God, and I was glowing.

At the end of the night, I got into the car exhausted, but I was not nauseous. I was not dizzy. I did not puke. I did not fall down. I was firm on the ground and neither my head nor eyes were in searing pain.

I called Matt who was excited but understandably a bit confused as I laid out the events that had unfolded. I went to sleep that night after a whirlwind of a day.

One night of feeling well didn't automatically cancel out almost five years of pain, dizziness, and nausea, so everyone around me entered that week cautiously and praying continually. I walked around in a blur—I completely trusted in God but also kept my hands open for the unexpected. A few women from my church fasted and prayed for me, but right away my mother and I sensed from God that we should praise Him rather than bring more prayer and petition. The week that ensued was unlike any I have ever experienced.

It started off with several of my mom's friends calling her out of the blue, saying they felt led to see how things were going with me. These friends didn't know anything about what had happened at the conference. One of our friends in particular called just days after the conference and told my mother that she had prayed for me every day for five years but that God had released her over the weekend, specifically from the burden she had for me. She had not been at the conference and apologized if I was doing terribly, but she said she just wanted my mom to know what she thought God was telling her.

I don't pretend to know how any of this works, but clearly God was communicating to those around me that I was healed without me even talking to them.

What was even crazier was that when I bumped into people who knew me well, they didn't recognize me. It wasn't everyone, but a few people noted that I indeed *looked* very different. One of my dad's friends, who I had known for my whole life, looked at me like he had never seen me before when I said hello. I explained this to a friend from school who was not professing to be a Christian, and I started to wonder why I was telling her this. I began to laugh because my story of being healed was already so spiritual and people not recognizing me seemed even *more* spiritual than that. However, she started losing color in her face as I spoke. She went on to explain that everything I said prior must be true because the entire time we were eating dinner, she knew something was different. She knew I was indeed her friend Jenna, but something had seriously changed and she couldn't quite pinpoint it. I looked different. I was touched by God, and everyone could literally see it.

My dad had a related experience, which was even more random than those of my mom. On the Tuesday after the conference, someone drove to my dad's family business to ask for a meeting with him to discuss something business-related. My dad never accepts business meetings without advanced scheduling, but for some reason he let it slide this time. As they spoke, the client mentioned something about his church in passing, and my dad asked him which church he attended. When my dad shared what church our family attended, the man lit up, exclaiming, "Do I have a story for you about that church!"

A couple that was dear to him had been expecting a new baby, but several weeks into the pregnancy they were told by their doctors that the baby would probably not survive because of a certain condition, and that they should consider an abortion. The man in my dad's office didn't attend my church, but he knew that a guest speaker was visiting and so he pleaded with the couple to go. The couple didn't normally go to church, but they didn't have anything to lose at that point. Amazingly, the guest speaker called on them during the service by name without knowing them, not unlike what I had experienced just three days before. The speaker went on to tell them their baby was going to be OK and they should re-run the tests. The baby was completely healthy, and the couple welcomed a new addition to their family months later.

In shock, my dad uttered, "Well, do I have a story for YOU about that church from three days ago!"

My dad recounted the events of the previous days to this person, and the man looked my dad in the eyes and said, "Your daughter is going to be OK." Welling up with tears, my dad knew God had sent this man to let my dad know it was real and that he could walk in faith that I was healed.

I was so grateful for these messengers of peace as I began to allow myself to believe that this could be my new normal.

Toward the end of that week, I felt moved to read about Elijah after he had prayed for rain. I opened up my Bible to 1 Kings 18:43-44, where we find Elijah sending his servant to check for the rain that he had prayed for:

"Go and look toward the sea," he told his servant. And he went up and looked.

"There is nothing there," he said.

Seven times Elijah said, "Go back."

The seventh time the servant reported, "A cloud as small as a man's hand is rising from the sea."

So Elijah said, "Go and tell Ahab, 'Hitch up your chariot and go down before the rain stops you.'"

I counted on my fingers. Seven people had spoken with my parents and shared in some way that God had confirmed that I was healed, without us prompting them. At this moment, God was asking me to have faith. I was feeling better, but I was overwhelmed. God had given me a cloud in the distance, and I was to run toward it with confidence.

One of the ways I did this was to attend my school's basketball game on Friday night. The team was in the Division III NCAA tournament, and my dad happened to get offered great seats in the front for me and my family. In the past, I might have chosen to attend out of fear of missing out on the fun, but it inevitably would have ended in me throwing up that night and being relegated to my bed for the rest of the weekend. This time, I decided to go because I was running toward what God had been telling me and my family all week. Sure enough, I enjoyed the whole game and our team won! My dad was offered tickets for the quarterfinals the next night, and I decided to go again.

After the first game, I told Matt about my night on his way back from the week-long research conference. He was excited to hear that I still seemed to be doing much better a week later and planned to go to the game with me the next night. I could tell that he was still cautious concerning what to think about my whirlwind of a week.

"Wow, and you're really feeling better?" he said hesitantly sitting on a bench miles away.

"I mean, yeah… I really, really am."

My mom and Matt always seemed to know how my injury would manifest itself, sometimes better than I even did.

As we were standing waiting to take our seats, Matt instantly and reflexively took a mental inventory of surrounding motion and sounds. Multiple basketballs flying different directions during warmups. Players running every which way. Cheerleaders calling out and dancing. People walking around, sitting down, standing up. My dad talking with one of his friends and introducing me. The scoreboard alarm going off. Any one or two of these would have been more than enough to send me careening for darkness and quiet and probably a toilet within seconds.

When the symptoms would start to take over, I would make eye contact with my mom or Matt, who always seemed to see it coming, and we would bow out of the situation. This time, Matt told me that he looked my way dozens of times out of concern, only to see me laughing and having a great time. He hadn't seen that since the accident, and he describes this as the moment that he knew I was healed. Our team ended up winning the game in spectacular fashion, and, more significantly, I had made it through all four quarters without a problem. My family and I celebrated along with everyone else in the stadium, although we were celebrating for another reason.

I saw the evidence of healing at the school event and attended two basketball games in faith, but something about the situation seemed distant to me. I was clinging on to pieces of evidential truth yet still felt guarded.

The next morning was church. This meant that I would be attending my third big outing of the weekend, which would have been unthinkable just a week prior. Since we were up late at the basketball game, we decided to go to the later service. That service was always louder and more energetic, so it was not an option we had considered since the injury. But that day, I walked through the doors into the sanctuary with confidence.

For the first time in a long time, my mind was not on symptoms at all; it was just on worshipping Jesus. I walked in holding Matt's hand as we sat with my family. We started singing "Reckless Love" and my arms went up in the air in worship.

I was overwhelmed by how amazing God is. I was caught up in the words of the song and all else faded away as it felt like it was only me in the sanctuary just worshipping at the feet of Jesus.

Then, in a moment, I realized everything had changed. Arms raised in the air and head held high, I looked into the blaring, blinking lights. I was not in pain. I watched all of the moving people around me and it did not make me dizzy. I was not nauseous at all. I had not even remembered what it felt like not to be nauseous. I did not feel like I was on a boat being tossed by the waves. I was steady.

The feelings of distance surrounding my healing were traded for the most personal feelings I have ever felt. God had touched my body, and now He was touching my soul.

I was healed.

It was really, truly, true, and I realized it all in one song.

I should've known it at the basketball games, but there was something so different about being back at church, standing before God, and Him releasing to me that it was all finally over.

I couldn't earn His healing, and I didn't deserve it, but He gave it to me. He gave me peace and filled my whole body with the truth that it was all over. Singing that song a week after the conference and sobbing my eyes out was the most powerful moment of my life.

I was steady on my feet in the church service. Usually I was crouched over in the seat, unable to lift my head up from between my knees, but that day I was no longer wincing in pain. I was OK.

I looked over at Matt. He was sobbing too. We were finally able to release the pain and stress of the years of struggling and open ourselves to believing that we had a new normal to live out. He said that even though he knew within seconds at the basketball game that I was completely physically different, something broke off in church. We were released to walk in faith that I was actually better.

My family was crying, and I was crying. I gave my mom the biggest and best hug. I hope I never forget that day. I wasn't just doing better; I was radically healed.

I was healed.

I was *healed*.

I was HEALED.

Looking back on my healing, two things stand out to me.

First, there was not anything intrinsically different that anyone did that day versus other times I had been prayed over. To the outside, those prayers were essentially the same ones that had been prayed over me for almost five years, with the same people who had prayed them with me many times, in the same church as before. I believe God gave those that prayed over me more wisdom this time, but He did not use different people. The speaker calling me out was unique, but I was still barely able to stumble out of the sanctuary after he had finished.

Second, this wasn't a time in my life that I was spending long spans of time reading the Bible or doing "spiritual" things. Like I said, I was spending more time watching early seasons of *Gilmore Girls* than reading my Bible (which obviously I do not recommend). It wasn't like my heart was noticeably closer to God this time than the other times I prayed to be healed.

To me, this meant that no other person was responsible for my healing, nor was I responsible. It was Jesus only.

For the trillionth time, God made it clear that His love is not earned through my actions or obedience and that He is in control of my story.

It reminded me that He didn't love me more or less before or after I was healed. He didn't love me more or less before or after the accident. He doesn't love me more or less based on anything I do. He doesn't love me because I love Him. He does not love me more when I am sick, and He does not love me more when I am well. He does not love me more when I witness to hundreds of people than when I sit and share my story with just one person. He just loves me.

Even as God was working a miracle in my mind and body, I almost felt like a third party to the whole process. The only thing I actually *did* was open myself up to God to have His way, while those around me prayed diligently with wisdom beyond my years.

It reminds me of the healing of the paralyzed man found in Mark 2. The friends of the paralyzed man brought him to Jesus, digging a hole through the roof and lowering him down to Jesus' feet. This was also my story. My family, my friends, my church, as well as people I hadn't even met slowly dug through the roof and lowered me down to Jesus' feet during all my years of sickness and injury.

Reading this story in the Bible, you may miss the fact that Jesus didn't actually heal the paralyzed man right away. When the man reached Jesus' feet, Jesus simply told him, "Son, your sins are forgiven." Jesus first healed the paralyzed man *internally*. He did the same with me. The first miracle God performed in my life was forgiving and healing my heart. He forgave me and healed me of my lack of trust, insecurity, fear, worry, and so many other things I could not get rid of on my own. God came in and took those things away through my complete surrender to Him. And just like the man in the second chapter of Mark (though it took a little longer for me), Jesus offered external healing as a physical manifestation of what He did in my soul.

Jesus asked a tough question in this story: "Which is easier: to say to this paralyzed man, 'Your sins are forgiven,' or to say, 'Get up, take your mat and walk'?" (Mark 2:9).

It seems to me it was harder to heal my identity than it was for God to heal me physically, even though there were years between the two. Before He healed me physically, God had *already* done the impossible of healing my heart.

Not drowning didn't mean the waves weren't crashing around me. It didn't mean I was not hurt. But as the waves attempted to pull me under, Jesus reached out His hand.

"Come and join me," (Matthew 14:29 TPT) Jesus tells us, as we look at His face. Hope is like oxygen to our souls. When we begin to look down and the earthly realities of the circumstance set in, we can feel suffocated beneath the waves. But when we look back to God, we know we won't drown because in life and death, we will be with Him.

As a child of God, *that* is who I am. *That* is my promised identity that will not change from this life until the next. My plans may change drastically, but *I* remain unmoved. My story isn't over, even when it looks that way. The riptides may pull me, but my purpose is never gone, even when it looks different.

As wave after wave crashed over my head,
I opened my eyes on the shore.
Seaweed and sand all stuck in my hair,
And my dad called to come back for more.

Crinkling my nose and squinting my eyes,
I knew what I had to do.
I would need to learn to swim in the waves,
And the lessons He told me rang true.

Just a bit older, yet young all the same,
The waves pushed me under their might.
Punching and losing my energy quickly,
I was never out of my Father's sight.

"Come and join me," Jesus called day after day,
I crinkled and squinted my face.
For sure the maker of the waves would stop them,
But rather, they stayed in their place.

"Will you trust me?" he said and I looked at his face
He gave me His arm to stop drowning,
I gave Him my hand and was pulled from the depths,
Walking on waves was shocking.

The waves still came as they do with the tides,
But the lesson I learned will remain.
I don't have to change when my plans do,
I am secure in sun and in rain.

As wave after wave crashed over my head,
I knew all along I'd survive.
The pain I endured had blinded my view,
But God is the God who provides.

EPILOGUE

Yesterday I went to the doctor for the first time since being healed. I told her that I was exponentially better, but I wanted her to do all of her tests before telling her why. Before this, my doctor was about to discharge me because of my slowing progress. I knew how much better I was doing qualitatively, but I was excited to see how this worked out quantitatively.

I prayed for boldness as I wondered how difficult it would be to share with her what happened. She was a world-class doctor who knew more about the brain and science than anyone I had ever spoken to. I knew that no matter how good or bad the appointment went, it would not move me, and I hoped it wouldn't shake me. I didn't want my story to be discounted by her, as she was finally the only doctor who took every symptom into consideration. I respected and revered her; she was a human hero in my mind. But I knew that even if the appointment went horribly, Jesus is so real. God loved this doctor so much, and even if it didn't go well, I rested in peace that He would use my story for His glory and purposes.

Previously, I scored "off the charts" low. This time, I was not afraid of what she would say, but I wanted her to see the results. Even if I needed more treatment, I knew I was on my way to recovery, with God as my champion. But as we worked through the tests, it was clear that things were different.

She started to tell me that whatever it was that was making me feel better had to be chemical. I needed physical transformation in my body before she could make any more progress with my vision and mental processing.

She did tests with a pen, then she did tests with a bell, and then color tests. Some with my eyes closed, and some with my eyes open.

"WOW!" she exclaimed. "You are way, way, WAY better."

My results all came back normal, as normal as someone could be. Rather than discharge me because I was too bad for her to help me anymore, she was going to discharge me because I didn't *need* help anymore.

I explained to her what happened without holding back a single detail. She was so happy for me as she processed all of what I was saying. After some time, she responded very seriously, "Wow, so this is a faith healing. I have only ever heard of a faith healing, but never seen one in person."

Toward the end of the appointment, she put down her tools. Taking a deep breath, she turned to my parents.

"You got your girl back."

I looked over at my parents on the side of the tiny room in Brooklyn. With tears in their eyes, they knew it was completely true *and* completely false. We would never get that eighteen-year-old girl back. I would never get my college years back. I could not think of anything worth that kind of pain other than the hope I have in Jesus. But it was true: in some ways, I was back.

I would have expected me to start crying in ecstasy because I could get back to being the old me again.

I did end up crying, but for a different reason. I cried because although I did not feel closure to the question of what my life has in store, I felt a deep sense of closure in my soul. A deep sense that this long, difficult battle was coming to an end.

After the doctor, we were very hungry and decided to stop for dinner in Manhattan on our way home. With tears in our eyes, we parked and walked to Tommy Bahama's new restaurant. I was walking on the street in New York City and standing fully upright. I didn't have to wear sunglasses, and I was not holding anyone's arm to stand tall. I was casually walking, and I was at peace. Everything around us was evidence of the miracle.

We entered the restaurant and must have all been beaming because the waiter exclaimed, "Celebrating, are we?"

We laughed and agreed, and he went to grab our sodas. My mom looked at my dad and me and asked, "So, are we going to tell him?" None of us were sure. None of us had ever been dramatically, physically healed by God before. We had no idea what that would look like in a casual conversation. We come from what we call "mainline Christianity." We know that God can heal because we believe that the Bible is true, but we had never seen someone touched by God in such a personally radical way.

Then my mom, answering herself, said, "Well, if you had just gotten into Harvard, we would tell him."

Knowing she was right, when the waiter came back I began to share with him why we were so excited. By the end of the meal, he brought his manager over and we all talked in the nearly empty restaurant as my parents and I enjoyed every dessert on the menu, on the house.

Sharing what Jesus did for me was as natural as talking about a close friend who had changed my life. It led our waiter and the manager to open up about their faith and where they were with God. It was a divine and special experience right in the center of Manhattan. Before I was healed, my purpose was to share what God had done for my soul despite my physical condition. Now after being healed, my purpose is still to share what God has done for my soul, evidenced by my new physical condition.

I believe I am here to mirror what Paul says: "I know what it is to be in need, and I know what it is to have plenty. I have learned the secret of being content in any and every situation, whether well fed or hungry, whether living in plenty or in want. I can do all this through him who gives me strength" (Philippians 4:12-13).

I used to think that verse meant I can set a goal and meet it with Christ's strength and help. Now I see it so differently. I now know it means no matter what comes our way in life, God will give us *His* strength to go on moment by moment if we rely on Him.

God is not a formula. I am OK with not knowing a formula that would explain why I suffered and why I had to lose my memory and years of my life. I am at peace with that unknown because of Christ who gives me true strength.

I woke up the morning of September 21, 2013, unable to read texts and unsure of what was wrong. Now, five years later, I am writing a book as I sit on a plane. Instead of constant symptoms, I feel a peaceful nothing in my body. I am *exhausted* from years of pain, but I have no severe symptoms. I am figuring out my new limits and gaining endurance in every which way of life. But more than anything, I am overwhelmed by God's love for me.

The riptide had spat me out on the sand, just like when I was a little girl. Squinting in the harsh sun I parted my hair, filled with seaweed and sand, away from my eyes to see where I was. What a long way I had come from where I had started.

I could not be more thankful that I had made it through the riptide. As I got up, I could finally see what a toll it had really taken on my body to fight for so long. I was physically weaker than before the waves had taken me, yet somehow much stronger.

"Come on back out!" God was calling to me from the sea.

I glanced in the direction of where I had first walked into the ocean. It was so far away! I had a choice. I could walk back up the beach and eventually find my way back to where I started. Or, I could dive back into the waves from where I was.

Acknowledgments

To those I have lovingly called Team Jenna, thank you from the bottom of my heart.

Mom, I am everything I am because you loved me. Thanks for being my strength, voice, and vision when I lost so much.

Dad, thanks for believing in me and supporting me in so many ways. I wouldn't be where I am without your prayers and steady love.

Matthew, the way you've loved me helps me gain deeper and greater understanding of how good God is. Thanks for your support in so many ways, and for helping me make this book a reality. Love you forever.

Cara, Jacob, and Carly, thank you for brightening up my days and for your support and love.

To my grandparents, thank you for never ceasing to pray for me. And my extended family, your consistent love, support, and gaze on Jesus has meant the world to me.

To everyone who was there for me when the lights went out – my doctors, therapists, friends, and church family, thank you for not giving up on me. They say it takes a village, thank you for being a part of mine: Leslie, Craig, Lauren, Shannon, Aura, Tara, Donne, Jeannine, Ash, Michele, Ruth Ann & Dave, Colin, Gail, Judy & Lou, Ray & Maureen, Debi, Anneke, Julia, Scoots, MJ, Don & Donna, Dr. Z, Amy, Mekina, and so many more.

AJ, you told me I could write the book myself and led me to Whitney, who I want to thank as well. Thank you both for believing in me and giving me the confidence to write it.

Kendall, thank you for spending quarantine with me and for tirelessly streamlining my long story. You helped me turn blog posts into a manuscript (without nearly as many "scare quotes"), and I still hear your voice as I write. I am so thankful for you.

Lindsay, thank you for stepping in at just the right time. You are one of a kind and such a crucial part of turning my manuscript into a book. I so appreciate your grace, hard work, and great insights.

Liz, thank you for partnering with me in the closing days. You are so talented and were such a great addition to the team.

Heather and team, thank you so much for helping me turn my book into a product I am proud of. Your advice, experience, and contributions were invaluable.

I wish I could hug each person who helped and was a part of this long journey. To the many amazing people not on this list, Thank You.

CHAPTER QUESTIONS

CHAPTER 1:

1. Have you ever been at the mercy of nature, caught in a riptide or a storm or something else? What did that feel like?

2. In everyday life, are you more likely to change your focus when you come against obstacles or power through even when you stop making progress?

3. How do you define "strength" in your life?

CHAPTER 10:

1. Do you become critical of yourself or doubt your abilities when someone you think you should be better than at something, succeeds more than you? What are a few ways you can stop the self-criticism cycle?

2. On the other side of comparison, do you sometimes use those less fortunate as a stepping-stone for thankfulness?

What is sacrificed when this is our primary response to pain in others? What could a more complete response look like?

3. When you are harsh or critical of yourself, how does this affect your ability to love and think of others? How can you separate this kind of self-centered frustration from normal sadness or feeling down?

4. You don't need what you don't have to fulfill God's plan for your life. What situations in your life does this truth speak to? How does it help in combating self-doubt and fear?

5. Is social media an unhealthy avenue of comparison in your life? How can you take part in the good things of social media without absorbing the toxic parts?

CHAPTER 11:

1. Are you the kind of person who likes change, or fears it? What about change makes you feel this way?

2. You don't need what you used to have to fulfill God's plan for your life. In what part of life does this speak to you?

3. How would everyday life be different if you immediately returned to truths about your worth in God whenever self-criticisms come in? How can you start to put this into practice?

CHAPTER 12:

1. Have you ever been in a situation where you were focused on hiding a weakness or insecurity from those around you? If God's power works best in weakness (2 Corinthians 12:9), how could this be getting in the way of God using you to bring good into that situation?

2. In what ways are you viewing your community more as a team than a body? How does the distinction of the body of Christ as a body rather than a team change how you see the value of your contributions?

3. Who are two people you could pray for and check in with right now? Take a few minutes to think and pray for them.

4. Why is sharing from personal experience sometimes so much more powerful than making arguments?

5. In what ways do you tend to escape your pain, fear, or uncertainty? How is inviting God into your situation different from you trying to escape?

CHAPTER 13

1. What are some "open doors" in your life that God may be asking you to walk through? How does the idea that "God equips the unequipped" free you up to say yes without fear?

2. Do you have a circumstance where obedience to God didn't result in earthly success? Were there ways you had to redefine success to come into better alignment with God's view of success?

CHAPTER 14:

1. After a traumatic life change, do everyday life events (like the baby shower in this chapter) challenge your faith?

2. How does living in faith and living in the world compare and contrast in your life right now?

3. Why is worry so tempting? What are three ways you can combat worry today?

CHAPTER 15

1. What labels are you holding on to that could be lost in a moment?

2. How can labels be dangerous?

3. How does this line from Chapter 15 resonate with you: "Everything I had worked for was taken away, but everything God had done in me remained intact"?

CHAPTER 16

1. When serving God, no time is wasted. Do you agree? How might someone in a "waiting period" be challenged by this thought?

2. Are you ready to answer the question: "How do *you* have hope?"

CHAPTER 17

1. Do you fall into the trap of believing that when things are easy, God is with you, but when things are hard, you

are on the wrong path? What is a helpful way to get out of this trap?

2. Where do you turn when you have tried everything and nothing seems to have worked?

3. Is there anything that you feel like God is calling you to go and do, but you are afraid to make the leap? What is one step you can take toward that this week?

CHAPTER 18

1. How do you balance praying for miraculous changes in circumstances with living in the purposes of your life exactly how it is today?

2. Is there anyone in your life with a tragic situation you could pray for? It may be too painful for them to pray for healing or deliverance for themselves.

3. Why is it hard to embrace the mystery of Jesus?

IF YOU READ NOTHING ELSE, READ THIS.

I could talk about my relationship with God until I am blue in the face, or write 100 more books about His love. But, the only way for you to experience the freedom and hope I found in Him (years before I was healed) is for you to start your own relationship with Him. It's hard to understand how a relationship with God can change your life unless you've experienced it. It's different than a prayer every so often to a God you think is there as you release good energy into the universe.

If you've never prayed before, here is a great place to start:

> Dear Jesus,
>
> I want to know You. I trust that You are the Lord of all creation and that You are good. Please come into my heart. I confess that I am in need of Your saving grace, and that I have turned against you and sinned in that way. Please forgive me. I believe You, Jesus, came to earth, died, and rose from the dead. I want to trust and follow You.

NEXT STEPS:

1. Trust that He heard you.

2. Get a Bible – a great place to start reading is the book of John.

3. Find Christian community/join a church.

> *If you declare with your mouth, 'Jesus is Lord,'*
> *and believe in your heart that God raised him*
> *from the dead, you will be saved."*
>
> ROMANS 10:9

Made in USA - North Chelmsford, MA
1284983_9780578982427
05.10.2022 1652